AMERICAN ESSAYS IN LITURGY

SERIES EDITOR, EDWARD FOLEY

FOUNDATIONS OF CHRISTIAN MUSIC: The Music of Pre-Constantinian Christianity

EDWARD FOLEY

 THE LITURGICAL PRESS
Collegeville, Minnesota

This work is a revised edition for the United States and Canada of the same title published in 1992 by Grove Books Ltd., Nottingham, England.

Illustrations on pages 34, 51, 69, and 92 by Robin Faulkner.

1   2   3   4   5   6   7   8

Library of Congress Cataloging-in-Publication Data

Foley, Edward.
    Foundations of Christian music : the music of pre-Constantinian Christianity / Edward Foley.
        p.   cm. — (American essays in liturgy)
    Includes bibliographical references.
    ISBN 0-8146-2396-4
    1. Church music—To 500.   I. Title.   II. Series: American essays in liturgy (Collegeville, Minn.)
    ML3003.F65   1996
    781.71'009'01—dc20   95-20948
                                                                CIP
                                                                MN

Contents

Abbreviations

EJ   *Encyclopaedia Judaica.* Eds. Cecil Roth and Geoffrey Wigoder. 16
            vols. Jerusalem: Keter Publishing House, 1972.

IDB   *The Interpreter's Dictionary of the Bible.* Ed. George Buttrick et al.
            4 vols. New York and Nashville: Abingdon, 1962.

Mishnah   All translations from *The Mishnah.* Trans. Jacob Neusner. New
            Haven and London: Yale University Press, 1988.

NGDMM   *New Grove Dictionary of Music and Musicians.* Ed. Stanley Sadie.
            20 vols. New York: W. W. Norton, 1980.

NJBC   *The New Jerome Biblical Commentary.* Eds. Raymond Brown,
            Joseph Fitzmyer, and Roland Murphy. Englewood Cliffs, N.J.:
            Prentice Hall, 1988.

NTA   *New Testament Apocrypha.* Eds. Edgar Hennecke and Wilhelm
            Schneemelcher. 2 vols. Trans. R. McL. Wilson. Philadelphia:
            Westminster Press, 1976.

TDNT   *Theological Dictionary of the New Testament.* Eds. Gerhard Kittel
            and Gerhard Friedrich. Trans. Geoffrey W. Bromiley. 10 vols.
            Grand Rapids: Eerdmans, 1964.

Introduction

For the student of liturgical music, the search for an adequate overview of Christian worship music in the first three centuries of the common era can be a daunting experience. There are many fine surveys of Church music, but few of them give much attention to the time before Constantine (d. 337). While there are numerous particular studies on various musical texts, practices, or personalities in the early Christian community, these seldom supply an adequate picture of the basic trends in early Christian worship or its music.

The reasons for this lacuna are multiple. The sources about worship in the first three centuries of the common era are quite fragmentary. There was little concern among the early believers to document their cultic or musical practices for later generations. What sources we do have provide little specific information about music, or contain information that is often allegorical and difficult to interpret. Yet more problematic than the sources is the question about the very nature of music within emerging Christianity.

In order for the contemporary inquirer to understand the music of pre-Constantinian Christianity it is necessary to think cross-culturally. The first Christians lived in a world very different from our own: a world not only dissimilar in time and geography, but distinctive in the ways that its inhabitants perceived and talked about reality. Any attempt to understand early Christian worship music, therefore, requires more than simply learning a new vocabulary or developing an ability to reconcile divergent texts about music in the ancient world. Rather, it compels us to think differently about music and its relationship to ritual. In doing so we will discover that some contemporary categories—such as distinctions between music and speech—are anachronistic frameworks that the ancients did not employ. Furthermore, many contemporary practices, such as our ability to celebrate worship without music, would be completely unintelligible to Christians of the first centuries. In order to enter into the world of early Christianity and comprehend the place and function of music in that world, we have to imagine and penetrate an auditory environment very different from our own.

Although there are many aspects of this ancient auditory environment that deserve our attention, none is more critical to the current study than the role of sound phenomena in divine revelation and worship. While contemporary Western society is visually oriented and believes what it sees, the first followers of Jesus—like their Jewish forebears—lived in a world where hearing was believing. Whether the interchange was a human affair or a divine-human dialogue, sound events were the prime mediator of presence and truth. This aural way of knowing deeply influenced the tonal landscape of early Christian worship which was as much a sonic as an optic event.

Before asking specific questions about early Christian music, therefore, we will first explore the tonal landscape of ancient Judaism and the New Testament world. This investigation will provide the necessary context for raising specific questions about "music" in early Christianity. After this preliminary investigation we will consider specific "musical" aspects of early Christian worship.

While there are many ways in which to organize such an investigation, I have chosen to organize the material according to the various places or types of places in which the followers of Jesus worshipped. We will begin with the Temple of Herod, then the synagogues of the first century, the borrowed spaces that characterized emerging Christianity in the first century, and finally the house churches of the second and third centuries. In each chapter we will describe the setting, and then attempt to answer questions about the type of "musicians" that functioned in that setting, the texts that might have been sung there, the manner of performing those texts, and the place of instruments in the worship. A brief summary will conclude each chapter.

Although there is much we do not know about the role of music in the emerging Christian community, there is an abundance of references, reconstructions, and hypotheses about the music of this era. There is no way that this slim volume can do justice to all of this material. Rather, what follows is intended as a guide to the central questions about the role of music in the emerging Christian community, as well as a credible survey of key primary and secondary sources about early Christian "music." Such historical considerations are foundational for those who wrestle with contemporary issues of liturgical music, and who need to befriend the tradition in order to respond adequately to the challenge of sung worship.

1 The Auditory Environment[1]

Oral Societies

While there are numerous ways in which to characterize societies of various ages, in terms of communication it is possible to divide cultures "into three successive stages: (1) oral or oral-aural, (2) script . . . and (3) electronic."[2] The fundamental distinction between stages one and two—between an oral and what might be called a proto-literate society—is that the former does not use any form of phonetic writing.[3] While an alphabet is not the only system which allows for phonetic transcription,[4] the presence of an alphabetic system does signal that a society has at least begun the transition out of its oral stage.

For those who wish to understand the nature of an oral society, Walter Ong offers an important caution: "the differences between oral-aural culture and our own technological culture are . . . so vast and so profound as to defy total itemization."[5] These differences are underscored by Ong's own limited itemization of some of the characteristics of an oral society, explanation of which is possible only by drawing negative parallels with contemporary experience. For example, Ong suggests that "one of the most striking and informative differences [between an oral culture and our own] is that an oral-aural culture is necessarily a culture with a relationship to time different from ours." In developing this concept, Ong relies almost exclusively on negative parallels to make his point: "[An oral-aural culture] has no records. It does have memory, but this is not by any means the same as records, for the written record is not a remembrance but an aid to recall. It does not belong to us as memory does. It is an external thing."[6]

Havelock proposes that one way to recognize the difference between our culture and an oral culture is by recognizing that in primary orality, relationships between human beings are governed exclusively by acoustics.

> The psychology of such relationships is . . . acoustic. The relation between an individual and his society is acoustic, between himself and his tradition, his law, his government. To be sure, primary communication begins visually with the smile, the frown, the gesture. But these do not get us very far. Recognition, response, thought itself, occur when we hear linguistic sounds and melodies and ourselves respond to them, as we utter a variant set of sounds to amend or amplify or negate what we have heard.[7]

While there are many other features of an oral society that one could enumerate,[8] this initial foray into cautions and characteristics alerts us to the radical differences between contemporary technological culture and the world of the ancient Near East.

Orality in Ancient Israel

In order for us to grasp something of the acoustic environment of ancient Israel we need to sketch in general terms when Israel was at the stage of primary orality and when, with the introduction of an alphabet and writing, it moved to the proto-literate stage. This necessitates the briefest of historical introductions to ancient Israel, followed by a similarly abbreviated overview of the history of alphabetic script in ancient Israel. These sketches will provide us with a framework for discussing the rise of writing within Israel, its movement from oral to written prophecy, the continuance of what might be termed "residual orality" as ancient Israel developed into a literate society, and allow some general comments about the dynamic nature of Hebrew language and thought. These historical-cultural reflections will allow us to gauge the auditory environment in Palestine in the first centuries of the common era, at the birth of Christianity.

An Historical Framework

The history of Israel[9] commonly begins with the patriarchal period, which Roland de Vaux suggests can be roughly dated to the first half of the second millennium B.C.E.[10] A second phase of Israel's early history is connected to the sojourn in Egypt and Joseph's rise to power (Gen 37–50).[11] A third phase encompasses the Exodus and Conquest events. The former, possibly involving two separate exoduses,[12] can be dated in the middle of the thirteenth century B.C.E. The latter—which was as much a period of coexistence, peaceful infiltration, and interdependence between the residents of Canaan and the Hebrew settlers as it was a time of conquest[13]—spanned the period slightly before the Exodus(es) until the mid-eleventh century B.C.E. The later part of the period of the Conquest is roughly coterminous with the age of the Judges. By the middle of the eleventh century B.C.E. a series of cultural and political developments gave rise to the monarchy in Israel. At the death of Solomon (922 B.C.E.) the kingdom was divided. The northern kingdom (Israel) fell to Assyria in 721 B.C.E.; the southern kingdom (Judah) fell to Babylon in 587 B.C.E.

A schematic of this history follows:

Patriarchal Period	ca. 2000–1700 B.C.E.
Sojourn in Egypt	ca. 1700–1300 B.C.E.?
entry of Semitic groups into Egypt	
the Joseph story	
Exodus and "Conquest"	ca. 1300–1050 B.C.E.
the Exodus(es)	ca. 1250 B.C.E.
the "Conquest"	ca. 1300–1050 B.C.E.
Age of the Judges	ca. 1200–1050 B.C.E.
Monarchy	ca. 1020–587 B.C.E.
division of kingdom	922 B.C.E.
fall of the northern kingdom	721 B.C.E.
fall of the southern kingdom	587 B.C.E.
Exile	587–539 B.C.E.

The Alphabet and Writing in Ancient Israel

It is possible that a Semitic alphabet[14] could have appeared as early as 1900 B.C.E.[15] The earliest extant Semitic texts are proto-Canaanite, dating from the seventeenth century B.C.E., from the region now known as Syria.[16] Proto-Canaanite and Canaanite scripts were succeeded by Old Phoenician (or North Semitic) script in the eleventh century B.C.E. The Israelites borrowed either a Phoenician or a similar Palestinian script (a sub-species of proto-Canaanite)—employed in Palestine before their arrival—sometime after the thirteenth century B.C.E.[17] Written Hebrew, properly speaking, has a single witness from the eleventh century B.C.E., and many more by the eighth century B.C.E.[18]

A schematic of this history[19] follows:

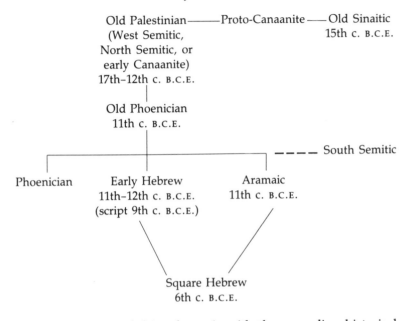

A comparison of this schematic with the preceding historical sketch suggests that writing entered the history of Israel very early. It is no coincidence that the refinement of Israel's national identity, symbolized in the rise of the monarchy, occurred in exactly the same period from which we have the first exemplars of Hebrew inscriptions.[20] It is possible that, since guilds of professional scribes existed in Egypt and Mesopotamia at this time,[21] the emerging monarchy borrowed this element of statecraft from Egyptian or Canaanite governmental models.[22] The emergence of Israel as a nation is intimately related to the emergence of the Hebrew language itself.

Writing, Scribalism, and the Deuteronomistic Movement

From the Old Testament we learn how widespread writing was among the Israelites. As de Vaux summarizes,

> Writing was in common use at an early date. Besides the professional scribes, like those employed at the court for administration (2 Sam

8:17; 20:25; 1 Kgs 4:3; etc.), and private secretaries like Baruch (Jer 36:4), members of the ruling class could write, judging by the stories of Jezabel (1 Kgs 21:8) and of Isaiah (Isa 8:1). But these were not the only ones: a young man of Sukkoth was able to give Gideon, in writing, the names of all the chiefs of his clan (Judg 8:14), and the commandment of Deut 6:9; 11:20 presumed that every head of a family could write.[23]

While writing entered Israel's history early, it did not serve as a primary means of communication or a central vehicle for the development of new theologies in ancient Israel. Thus, while sections of the Pentateuch were put into writing in the tenth century B.C.E.,[24] these elements did not originate as written texts and retained what might be called a residual orality.[25] This situation began to change, however, in the seventh century B.C.E.

In the eighth and seventh centuries B.C.E. Assyria was a major military force in the Near East, dominating both the northern and southern kingdoms. Under the influence of the Assyrian Empire, which greatly valued the role of the professional scribe,[26] scribalism flourished throughout the Near East to the extent that this is sometimes characterized as a "scribal age."[27] In Israel this trend came to fruition in the emergence of the Deuteronomistic movement.

It is hardly coincidental that the Deuteronomistic movement arose within this period. The written incorporation of historical traditions and legal codes by Deuteronomists parallels this increasingly prominent role of the scribe. This is evident in the Biblical portrayal of the Josianic Reform, which symbolizes the Deuteronomistic movement itself (2 Kgs 22). Here, it is the written word that is the basis for the king's conversion. Likewise, it is a scribe—Shaphan—who is accorded a primary place in the discovery (22.3), the handling (22.8), and the interpretation (22.14) of the scroll. From this point on the written traditions will be an increasingly important component in the cultic life of Jerusalem.[28]

While the Deuteronomists are pivotal for giving written shape to the Law, their influence on proto-literate Israel extends further, into prophetic literature. It is this development which becomes determinative for identifying the Word of God with the written word in ancient Israel.

From Oral to Written Prophecy

Around the time of the Deuteronomistic movement a revolution was taking place in prophetic literature.[29] As M. B. Dick suggests, this revolution entailed the increased incorporation of written passages in prophecy, which in essence and origin was an oral medium. This conclusion is based on R. Coote's work on the Book of Amos[30] which demonstrates that one stratum of Amos (Amos A) reflects the existence of orally delivered oracles while a second stratum (Amos B) suggests prophecy that was never orally delivered but was a written composition. Dick concludes that, because of the resemblance of Amos B to the Deuteronomist, it can be dated to the late seventh century.[31]

The work of the prophet Jeremiah stands at a pivotal moment in the transition from oral to written prophecy. Jeremiah 36 describes the production of a written prophetic document.[32] What is unusual in this account, however, is that oral prophecy and scribal transmission—separate processes in the Book of Amos—now appear to converge. "Either during his lifetime or shortly thereafter, [Jeremiah's] oracles, and the accounts of many incidents within his life, were committed to writing."[33] While the reasons for this convergence are not yet agreed upon, the result of this process is that the written word is identified with the word of the Lord.[34]

By the post-exilic period, prophecy was more and more a written endeavor.[35] Dick suggests that the Book of Chronicles provides a *terminus ad quem* for this transition. "By the time of the Chronicler, a contemporary of Haggai and Zechariah (ca. 520 B.C.E.), prophecy was already presumed to be written."[36]

Residual Orality in Ancient Israel

The appearance of a Hebrew alphabet, the rise of scribalism and the convergence of oral prophecy and scribal transmission in Jeremiah all attest to the gradual transformation of ancient Israel from a proto-literate to a craft- or even semi-literate society. Even the dominance of written prophecy in post-exilic Israel, however, does not mean the end of Israel as an oral society, for the transition from one stage of orality to another takes centuries to achieve.[37] Thus, while writing might have been widespread among the Israelites before the Exile, de Vaux himself—who treats writing within the larger framework of education—concludes that most teaching was done by word of mouth.[38]

It was not only education that maintained an "auditory bias" in ancient Israel. Many of the characteristics of this pre-literate state endured for centuries. The primary source for discovering these characteristics is the Old Testament. While it is true that the Old Testament was redacted by a society at least at the stage of craft-literacy, the texts themselves exhibit what Havelock calls "concealed oralism."[39] As he explains, concealed oralism is a way of acknowledging that "genuine echoes from a primary orality long forgotten have been retained intermittently in a text otherwise devoted to revising them, epitomizing them, and incorporating them in a theological framework devised by a written tradition."[40] While there are a number of indicators of this "concealed oralism" in the Old Testament, a brief consideration of three of them should make the point.

1) *The Dominance of Auditory over Visual Imagery in Divine Manifestations.* It is generally true that auditory images dominate the stories of divine manifestation in the Old Testament. This can be demonstrated in a number of ways.

First, there is what might be called the preparatory nature of the visual manifestation of God in the Old Testament. As Gerhard Kittel notes, accounts of seeing God in the Hebrew Scriptures simply provide the setting for the revelation of the word that follows as, for example, in the vision of the prophet Isaiah (6:1ff.) or Ezechiel (1:1ff.). "When God appears, it is not for the sake of the theophany, but in order . . . to cause Himself to be heard indirectly or directly. The decisive religious statement is: 'Hear the Word of the Lord' (Isa 1:10; Jer 2:4; Am 7:16)."[41]

Second, the divine presence is often visually obscured, so that God is never adequately or completely seen. Samuel Terrien elucidates this point: "Either there is too much light, in which case the storytellers emphasize the blinding quality of the experience, or there is too little light—the experience occurs in the gloom of night or in a cloud of total darkness—and the storytellers pile up synonyms for obscurity in order to stress divine invisibility."[42] Thus, for example, in the previously noted divine "vision" of Ezechiel, the prophet describes the Lord's appearance (Ezek 1:28b) "like the appearance of fire enclosed round about; and downward from what had the appearance of his loins I saw as it were the appearance of fire, and there was brightness round about him. Like the appearance of the bow that is in the cloud on the day of rain, so was the appearance of the brightness round him" (Ezek 1:27-28a). The prophet himself calls this "the likeness of the glory of the Lord" (Ezek 1:28b) more than a vision of God.

Third, a true vision of God is something both exceptional and dangerous in the Hebrew Scriptures.[43] Thus, when Moses realized that the Lord God was revealing Godself in the burning bush, "Moses hid his face, for he was afraid to look at God" (Exod 3:6). Later in Exodus God announced to Moses that, though God will "make all my goodness pass before you . . . you cannot see my face; for man shall not see me and live" (Exod 33:19-20). While it is true that in some cultic contexts "to see Yahweh" often had the positive meaning of experiencing the presence of God in the Temple (for example, Pss 42:3; 84:8; Isa 38:11), in other contexts, such as Exodus 33, it could be life-threatening. When Isaiah saw Yahweh in the Temple he feared for his life (Isa 6:5) and when Amos saw the Lord in his fifth vision (Amos 9:1) destruction and death ensued.[44]

Closely related to this pattern in which auditory imagery prevails over visual imagery in divine manifestation is the ban against visual depictions of God at the heart of Israel's law (Exod 20:4; Deut 5:8). The aniconic tradition in Israel is not only ancient, but also without a real parallel in the ancient Near East.[45] While it is true that a variety of graphic designs, images, and decorations did grace various Jewish buildings,[46] "no certain image of Yahweh has so far been found at any Israelite site."[47]

The one great exception to these generalizations about visions of God comes from Exodus 24:9-11. In this unusual passage, God was seen directly by humans who actually ate and drank with God: "And they saw the God of Israel; and there was under his feet as it were a pavement of sapphire stone like the very heaven for clearness. And he did not lay his hand on the chief men of the people of Israel; they beheld God, and ate and drank." As if to emphasize the point, the passage twice reports that Moses and his companions saw God. Terrien suggests that this story is "without parallel in the Hebrew tradition" and was shocking to Hellenistic Jews who added the phrase "God is not seen, only the place where he stood" to verse 10.[48] While this text is extreme it does represent a pattern in stories of divine revelation that emerged from the southern tradition—although it is not clear that this story itself had such an origin. This pattern, as Terrien describes it, is one in which southern theologians increasingly interpreted divine presence and divine revelation through the theologoumenon of the glory.[49] However, this is a later development in the history of ancient Israel; the emphasis on the preparatory, obscuring, and dangerous nature of visual encounters with the divine seems to be older and foundational.[50]

16

2) *The Importance of the Organs for Hearing and Speaking.* There are three different ways in which the Old Testament stresses the organs for hearing and speaking. First, these Scriptures emphasize that the ear and hearing are constitutive for an authentic definition of personhood. The ear is sometimes seen as a merely physical organ, but the figurative reference to the ear "as a symbol of the complete process of hearing and, by extension, of understanding and obedience is far more significant."[51] An introduction to the role of the ear and hearing in the Hebrew Scriptures is provided by Eliphaz who articulates how, starting from the ear, the whole person is activated (Job 4:12-14).[52] To "open someone's ears" (Isa 48:8) or to "awaken someone's ears" (Isa 50:4) are basic expressions for communicating with another. Other texts from the First Testament suggest that hearing determines one's behavior and state of being generally (for example, Gen 3:8-10). It is an organ not simply for acquiring auditory information, but for understanding and receptivity. In some instances, the ear serves as a parallel for the heart (Prov 2:2; 18:15; 23:12), which is the seat of the whole inner life.[53] Thus, Solomon asks for a heart that hears so that he might be able to discern between good and evil (1 Kgs 3:10); the ear becomes the fundamental metaphor for Solomon's wisdom.[54] These and other examples demonstrate that hearing is constitutive of the whole, developed individual.[55]

Second, the Old Testament emphasizes that the ear and hearing are essential for an authentic relationship with God. Besides serving as a critical means for achieving personhood, the ear and hearing provide a fundamental link between humans and God. In ancient Israel God was more often heard than seen. Besides the simple quantity or dominance of such passages, the Hebrew Scriptures further demonstrate that without the capacity to hear—literally and metaphorically—humankind would be severely disabled in its ability to sustain a relationship with the God of Israel. From the beginning, God has initiated the dialogue: be that at the mythic beginning of time (Gen 1:26-30), the beginning of the covenant with Abraham (Gen 12:1-3), or when Yahweh took charge of the existence of Israel (Exod 23:22).[56] Not only does God speak, but God speaks a law that humans are called to hear and obey. The biblical expression for obeying is to "listen to" God, to God's voice (Gen 3:17; 28:7). To obey God (Isa 42:24) or to obey God's law (Jer 9:12) requires first that one hear God,[57] and then act. Since God has created the ear (Prov 20:12) humans have a great responsibility to use their ears wisely, allowing God to open them so that life can be aligned with reality.[58] This point is dramatically made in the daily confession known as the Shema (Deut 6:4-9; 11:13-21; Num 15:37-41), which begins "Hear, O Israel." Thus Kittel concludes that an essential feature of biblical religion is that, "It is a religion of the Word, because it is a religion of action, of obedience to the Word. The prophet is the bearer of the Word of Yahweh which demands obedience and fulfillment. Man is not righteous as he seeks to apprehend or perceive God by way of thought and vision, but as he hears the command of God and studies to observe it."[59] More than any other sense perception, hearing provides the vital link between the God of Israel and humankind.

Third, the Old Testament employs an extended vocabulary for the organs of speech. Since the received word is incomplete without a response,[60] and the organs of speech articulate that response, the First Testament gives these organs special attention. "Whereas the ear and the eye only have one word each in the Old Testament, a whole collection of parts of the body represent the instrument of speech."[61] The mouth (*peh*) is the main organ of speech. As the organ that expresses what the ear and eye have perceived, it distinguishes humans from all other creatures and stands quite near to humankind's essential being.[62] Other parts of the body that represent the instrument of speech include:[63] *s 'āpā* which literally means "lips" (Ps 22:8), but also is a metaphor for language (Isa 6:7); *lāson*, the "tongue" (Lam 4:4), but also a figure for true (2 Sam 23:2) or false (Ps 12:3) speech; *ḥek* or "palate," literally the seat of the sense of taste (Ps 119:103); *gāeōn*, at once the "throat" (Jer 2:25), but also an organ of speech (Isa 58:1).

3) *The Dynamic Nature of the Hebrew Language and Hebrew Thought.*
A third indicator of concealed oralism in the Old Testament is what Thorlief Boman calls the dynamic nature of the Hebrew language and thought. This dynamism is demonstrated by the dynamic character of Hebrew verbs of inaction. According to Boman, Hebrew verbs always tend to express movement or activity.[64] This is most striking in verbs of inaction such as "standing" (*natsabh*), "sitting" (*vashabh*), or "stretch out" (*shakhabh*). While indicating a position of repose or inactivity, in the Hebrew mind such experiences of stasis were related to the motion that preceded them. Boman concludes that "motionless and fixed being is for the Hebrews a nonentity; it does not exist for them."[65] He draws a similar conclusion about

18

verbs of condition and quality such as "to be/become angry" (*'aneph*), or "to be/become bright" (*'ôr*),[66] as well as the verb "to be" (*hayah*).[67] Claude Tresmontant concurs when considering the nature of understanding (*bina*) in the prophetic writings: "What the prophets call understanding, *bina*, is not a faculty, an *organon* endowed with certain a priori categories, a power that would pass into action under certain circumstances. Understanding *is* action, the act of intellection of subsistent truth. Hebrew, a concrete language, never speaks of understanding except in such a context of truth's fruition."[68]

Boman concludes that for the Hebrews, the world itself possessed an active character, and was always in motion.[69]

Orality in Emerging Christianity

The Hellenistic Context

Almost four centuries before the birth of Christ, Alexander the Great (d. 323 B.C.E.) conquered the whole of the eastern Mediterranean world. Alexander also transformed the Near East by imposing his own culture and language upon the peoples he subdued. Although the empire was divided among Alexander's generals after his death, the influence of his Hellenizing campaign continued for centuries. This was true even in Palestine, where the Jews did not reestablish their political independence until almost 150 years after the death of Alexander. Although they attempted to assert their cultural independence from Hellenism as well, this effort was short lived and ultimately unsuccessful. Rome conquered the Jewish monarchy in 63 B.C.E. and continued the process of Hellenization. Thus it was in a Jewish milieu under the political and cultural influence of the Greco-Roman world that Christianity emerged.

The culture that Alexander exported from Greece was one in which seeing rather than hearing was celebrated as the most important human sense. This development occurred between the time of Homer (before 700 B.C.E.) and Plato (d. 347 B.C.E.). Although Greek culture at the time of Homer was not without writing, and at the time of Plato was not without epic poetry or oral performance, in the later period the emphasis was clearly shifting from the ear to the eye. It was not Plato who initiated this change. In his writings there is a general absence of argument on the subject and he simply seems to take for granted the preeminence of vision.[70] He does, however, become the great prophet of visualization[71] and after him there is little doubt that vision is held to be the most excellent of the senses. The influence of Plato and the philosophy that emerged from a society that valued seeing over hearing was extensive and pervasive. Ultimately it provided a framework for Western civilization that would allow the assertion that seeing is believing.

Despite this powerful Hellenistic influence, in the ancient world in general—and in Palestine in particular—hearing continued to dominate. Although segments of the culture communicated significantly through literary means,[72] the culture of late Western antiquity was what Paul Achtemeier calls "a culture of high residual orality."[73] One irrefutable symbol of this was the continued practice of reading aloud. "The oral environment was so pervasive that no writing occurred that was not vocalized . . . even solitary readers, reading only to themselves, read aloud."[74] Thus it appears that the Hellenized world that provided the context for the emergence of Christianity, maintained a distinctive auditory environment in which orality was highly valued.

Hellenized Judaism, in particular, continued as a culture with high residual orality. While there are many symbols of this around the time of Christ, particularly significant is the growing importance during this period of the oral Torah (*Torah she-b'al peh*). The Pharisees were a small group within Palestinian Judaism that emerged during the period of the second Temple. They distinguished themselves from other Jews by claiming that,

> when God revealed the Torah to Moses at Mount Sinai, God gave the Torah in two parts. One part was in writing . . . the other part was not written down, but was meant to be handed on through memorization and repetition of the precise language that had been memorized from one generation to the next. This other half of the Torah is called, therefore, the Oral Torah, or the Torah which is memorized.[75]

Between ca. 200 B.C.E. and 100 C.E. the Pharisees strongly asserted their right to rule all the Jews by virtue of their possession of this oral Torah.[76] Eventually they succeeded in wresting spiritual leadership in Palestinian Judaism away from the Sadducees who did not believe in these claims about the oral Torah. The Pharisees' growing influence with its reassertion of the oral component of the Law effectively underscores the sensitive auditory environment of first-century Palestinian Judaism, and its continued emphasis on orality.

The Jesus Experience

Just as one cannot consider the oral nature of emerging Judaism apart from its cultural context, so one cannot understand the auditory aspects of the Jesus experience apart from Palestinian Judaism at the beginning of the common era. Jesus was a Jew and part of a culture and religious tradition that valued hearing as much if not more than seeing—especially in the transmission of religious truths. This auditory awareness, common to all Palestinian Jews of the period, seems to have been especially forceful for Jesus because of particular geographic and linguistic circumstances. Greek was the language that, more than any other in the ancient Near East, served as a vehicle for the ascendancy of sight over sound in Western thought. One can surmise, however, that because Jesus was a Jew from rural Palestine whose first language was Aramaic, the Hellenistic tendency to prize the visual over the auditory was somewhat muted.

We have already noted how teaching in Judaism was essentially an oral enterprise.[77] As a teacher, Jesus was inevitably engaged in this auditory venture. While it is true that some rabbis did employ writing as a way to communicate their teachings, there is no evidence that Jesus ever did so, even though he could read (Luke 4:16ff.) and write (John 8:6). Jesus' reliance on oral instead of written communication may have been a conscious choice. The basis for any such choice would have been an awareness of oral communication's "greater power for reaching and transforming the people of the day."[78]

Was Jesus unique in this regard, or might his preaching style simply have been similar to that of other rabbis of his day? [79] Holding the latter position would seem to ignore a radical difference between the speech of Jesus and that of other Jewish teachers—a difference that has its own theological significance.[80] Amos Wilder emphasizes the extemporaneous nature of Jesus' speech: not carefully crafted or methodically thought out beforehand, but ingeniously improvised in a specific context. According to Wilder, Jesus' speech was naïve, not studied: "It is extempore and directed to the occasion, it is not calculated to serve some future hour. This utterance is dynamic, actual, immediate, reckless of posterity; not coded for catechesis or repetition."[81]

If Wilder's analysis is accurate, then Jesus, unlike other rabbis of first-century Palestine, "was not schooling his followers in a learned mode that could be passed on to future generations. Rather, he spoke to the immediate crisis of the day in a free and spontaneous style."[82] And it was a particular crisis of his day that demanded this new style of speech-act.[83]

As an eschatological prophet,[84] Jesus was aware that the kingdom was in the process of being revealed.[85] While there were those in Palestinian Judaism whose primary expressions of eschatological hope were written, "there was another stratum of society whose hopes were expressed in a more 'activist,' even 'revolutionary' manner."[86] Jesus' eschatological message, understood in this context, was a dynamic and revolutionary speech-act that eschewed writing. "The act of writing presupposes continuities and a future . . . [but for Jesus] and his generation, history was fractured, time's course was in dissolution, continuities were broken. Jesus' word was for the present, the last hour."[87] Thus his examples are realistic and vivid—deftly chosen from existential experience.[88] This immediacy of language well serves the eschatological message in a style that is unique and memorable. As Wilder summarizes,

> The incomparable felicity and patterning of his sayings is indeed evident, but this formal perfection is not a matter of mnemonics; it is the countersign of the most effective communication of the moment. Naturally his words and parables were remembered and retold, often with great accuracy, so lucid and inevitable was his phrasing. But here as always the new speech of the Gospel was not a matter of words on a table but a word in the heart, not a copybook for recitation but winged words for life.[89]

Thus could David Tracy suggest that the New Testament sayings of Jesus, especially his reported parables, are a kind of "limit-language." According to Tracy, Jesus' language transgresses the ordinary apocalyptic language and, in the process, a new disclosure occurs. " 'Another' world opens up: not an apocalyptic, super-everyday world; but a limit dimension to this world, this experience, this language."[90] Tracy, like others, sees this happening especially in the parables. "The parables, as stories, take the reader to the point where the course of ordinary life is broken; an intensification of the everyday emerges; the unexpected happens; a strange world of meaning is projected which challenges, jars, disorients our everyday vision precisely by both showing us the limits to the everyday and projecting the limit-character of the whole."[91]

Jesus the rabbi embodied the Jewish predilection for orality over visualization, the speech-act over writing. As an eschatological prophet, he not only relied upon a heightened auditory environment, but transformed it through revolutionary forms of speech that could not be contained by writing. And, as the Word made flesh, he proclaimed and embodied the word so uniquely that the kingdom was revealed in a singular and unrepeatable articulation.

The Oral Kerygma

Jesus' revolutionary style of preaching evoked a similar revolution in the language of his disciples. Although the early community was concerned to hand on Jesus' teaching, they did not persuade people to believe in Jesus by repeating his teachings (*didachē*), but through preaching (*kerygma*)—an act that had more in common with town criers or auctioneers than traditionally understood rabbinic discourse.[92] "Although Christianity from the very beginning had a scripture, the Hebrew Scriptures, the faith of the earliest Christians was evoked by and focused on a person, Jesus of Nazareth. Jesus, in the earliest Christian communities, was known not in Bible texts but in missionary preaching, oral tradition and charismatic experience."[93]

It is from this perspective that Ernst Fuchs can suggest that primitive Christianity itself was a speech-phenomenon[94] that did not first concern itself with written forms. Rather, in the memory and example of Jesus, the first disciples went about proclaiming the good news, and in so doing contributed to a heightened auditory environment in which Jesus was proclaimed. It is this oral performance that lay at the heart of the early Christian message, and generated the new religious form of truth known as the gospel. It was only through this auditory kerygma—what Frederick Crowe calls "gospeling the gospel"[95]—that belief was possible.[96]

Residual Orality in the New Testament

With increasing frequency scholars are approaching the New Testament not simply as a collection of literary works but as attempts by various communities to translate into writing what was essentially an auditory phenomenon. The Gospel of Mark, for example, is dominated by the oral form of storytelling.[97] Indeed, all of the New Testament documents ''are oral to the core, both in their creation and in their performance.''[98] Rooted in the free oral dialogue of Jesus and his disciples, which was memorized and repeated for believers, the stories and parables were eventually written down. ''But even when the face-to-face rhetorical forms of the beginnings gave way to the conventionality of written records and letters, these are still characterized by a perennially dramatic element which goes back to the very nature of the Christian religion. The Christian styles tend to evoke or restore the face-to-face encounter.''[99]

Like the Hebrew Scriptures, the New Testament preserves many traces of residual orality. This ''concealed oralism'' is much more prominent in the New Testament than in the Hebrew Scripture as the time between the oral event and written form for the former is far more condensed than that same process for the latter. While there are a number of indicators of the New Testament's concealed orality, a brief consideration of three of them should make the point.

First is the emblematic role of parables in the New Testament. As Edward Schillebeeckx and others have noted, Jesus not only taught in parables but himself was a parable.[100] His parables were intimately wed to his announcement of the kingdom.[101] They were certainly one of the most characteristic story forms employed by Jesus. Kelber reminds us that the ''oral propriety of parabolic stories requires little argument.''[102] Parables are oral forms that presume and require the speech-event for their power. Even when they are translated into written forms, they retain various oral characteristics, such as certain mnemonic devices.[103] In the Gospel of Mark, for example, both the parable of the sower and that of the mustard seed employ the mnemonic device of contrast, which renders these stories ''orally impressionable.''[104] Paul Ricoeur has suggested that another characteristic of many parables is what he terms ''extravagance.''[105] According to Kelber, this concept further illuminates the mnemonic process of parables. ''Over and above the mnemonic patterning, it is the element of excess and irregularity that eases remembering. The trivial facilitates identification, but oddness makes these stories memorable. For what one remembers is not the pane in the window, but the crack in the pane.''[106]

The residual orality of the New Testament is also demonstrated by the dominance of auditory over visual imagery for revelation and faith. Although the verbs of seeing outnumber the verbs of hearing in the New Testament, this does not mean that seeing is the more important of the senses. It is true that at some moments, particularly in the Gospel of John, seeing is more highly esteemed than hearing (John 8:38).[107] In general, however, at moments of revelation or faith "there can be no doubt as to the primacy of hearing."[108] Even when the New Testament depicts revelatory events in visual terms, such events usually acquire their true significance through what is heard. For example, the appearance of the angel at the annunciation acquires its true significance through the accompanying message (Luke 1:28-37), the baptism of Jesus acquires its true significance with the voice heard afterward (Mark 1:11), and the transfiguration acquires its true significance with the revelatory word (Matt 17:5). As Wilder summarizes,

> The New Testament speaks of the divine apprehension in terms of all the senses, not only hearing and sight but touch and smell (the last in the form of incense and fragrant odours). Yet the hearing mode is primary. The spirit may be rapt in vision, but it is with the heart that man hears the word of faith and with his mouth that he confesses and is saved (Rom 10:8-10). Language, then, is more fundamental than graphic representation, except where the latter is itself a transcript in some sense of the word of God.[109]

A further testimony to the oral genesis and foundation of the New Testament is the existence of numerous parallel passages that are yet markedly different from each other. No example of this is more striking than that of the institution narratives.[110] While there is a core of material that is common to the four institution narratives recorded in the New Testament—both in structure[111] and in text[112]—there is yet enormous diversity between these citations.[113] This diversity can best be explained by what Jeremias calls "a living process of growth in the tradition."[114] At the basis of these varying texts was an historical, oral event. This event served as the basis for the liturgical practice of emerging Christianity. It was the liturgical context—the cultic speech-event of emerging Christianity—that gave rise to the parallel yet diverse institution accounts imbedded in the New Testament. The institution narratives are one example of residual orality, in which oral transmission and enactment generated written texts. The residual orality of the institution narrative continues to be affirmed by various segments of Christianity which over the centuries have employed variations on the biblical texts in ritual enactment.[115]

Summary

This brief introduction to the dominance of auditory over visual imagery in divine manifestations, the importance of the organs for hearing and speaking and the dynamic nature of the Hebrew language and Hebrew thought as revealed through the Old Testament suggests that, despite the fact that writing might have been widespread, there continued what might be called an "auditory bias" in ancient Israel. This observation finds a corollary in the work of Jack Goody who asserts that "the division between 'literacy' and 'orality' is never a question of crossing a single frontier, a simple binary shift."[116] Rather, as Goody notes, even literary composition requires oral or sub-oral processes. Thus, while the Old Testament was redacted by a society at least at the stage of craft-literacy, the texts exhibit the kind of concealed oralism that allows us to assert the auditory bias of Hebrew life and thought.

At the dawn of Christianity, this heightened auditory environment endured, despite Hellenizing influences that valued seeing over hearing. For Jesus, in particular, the spontaneous word-event was a fundamental characteristic of his ministry. Announcing the immediacy of the good news in a manner "reckless of posterity"[117] typified his public ministry, and that of his followers. Despite the emergence of written forms like the gospel, a primacy of audition continued to characterize developing Christianity. For the early Christians, hearing was believing.

There have been few explicit references to music in this chapter, much less the music of ancient Christianity, which is the prime concern of this monograph. Before explicitly addressing the topic of music, however, some acknowledgement and understanding of the broader sonic environment of the ancient Near East, Judaism, and emerging Christianity are essential.[118] As has been noted before, and will be noted again, twentieth-century Western concepts of music do not necessarily provide an adequate framework for understanding what another culture or another time might consider music or musical. This is especially true when people from a visually dominated tradition attempt to raise musical questions about an oral society. Appreciating something of the nature of an auditory environment in general, and the auditory environment of the movement or culture under investigation in particular, is the first step in gaining such understanding.

CHAPTER ONE NOTES

1. "Auditory environment" and "acoustic environment" are terms that are meant to demonstrate a concern not simply or essentially for an individual sound or musical event, but for the physical, historical, and cultural environment that shapes the perception and understanding of such individual sounds or musical events. The terms are somewhat analogous to those of "soundscape" or "sonic environment" coined by F. Murray Schafer. See, for example, the definitions Schafer offers in his glossary of *The Tuning of the World* (New York: Alfred Knopf, 1977) 274–75, and passim.

2. Walter Ong, *The Presence of the Word* (New Haven: Yale University Press, 1967) 17. Eric Havelock offers a refinement on this three-part schema by suggesting that the first stage of a culture is that of primary orality, followed by the proto-literate, the craft-literate, the semi-literate, and the fully literate stages (Eric Havelock, *The Muse Learns to Write: Reflections on Orality and Literacy from Antiquity to the Present* [New Haven and London: Yale University Press, 1986] 65).

3. It should be noted that the common application of the term *writing* to any and every form of symbolization without distinction blurs the boundaries between the various stages of a society's development; see Havelock, *The Muse Learns to Write*, 65.

4. Jack Goody, *The Interface between the Written and the Oral* (Cambridge: Cambridge University Press, 1987) 38–41.

5. Ong, *The Presence of the Word*, 23.

6. Ibid.

7. Havelock, *The Muse Learns to Write*, 65–66.

8. The following list is distilled from Ong, *The Presence of the Word*, 22–35 and Havelock, *The Muse Learns to Write*, 63–78: (1) in an oral society communication, even between individuals, has an aspect of a social phenomenon; (2) oral societies rely on the narrative format for memorizing and transmitting fundamental truths; (3) tradition is taught by action, not by idea or principle; (4) the oral audience participates not merely by listening passively but by active participation—they clap, dance and sing collectively in response to the chanting of the singer; (5) an oral society has no history in the modern sense of that term; (6) an oral society nourishes memory skills beyond those cultivated in present-day technological societies; (7) in oral societies ritualization becomes the means of memorization; and (8) in oral societies words are more celebrations and less tools than in literate cultures. For a cautionary note on comparing literate to non-literate societies, see Ruth Finnegan, "Literacy versus Non-literacy: The Great Divide?" in *Modes of Thought: Essays on Thinking in Western and Non-Western Societies*, ed. Robin Horton and Ruth Finnegan (London: Faber and Faber, 1973) 112–44.

9. See the accessible outline by Addison Wright and Roland Murphy in NJBC 75:5–144; this outline provides the basis for the historical reconstruction which follows.

10. Roland de Vaux, *The Early History of Israel,* trans. David Smith (Philadelphia: Westminster Press, 1978) 266.

11. While it appears that certain Semitic groups entered Egypt sometime in the middle of the second millennium B.C.E., the historicity of the Joseph story is disputed. See, for example, Siegfried Herrmann, *A History of Israel in Old Testament Times,* 2d ed. (Philadelphia: Fortress Press, 1981) 56.

12. De Vaux, *The Early History of Israel,* 363–87.

13. See, for example, David Noel Freedman and David Graf, eds., *Palestine in Transition,* The Social World of Biblical Antiquity, series editor James W. Flanagan (Sheffield: Almond Press, 1983); especially Marvin L. Chaney, ''Ancient Palestinian Peasant Movements and the Formation of Premonarchic Israel,'' 39–90.

14. These were what Goody calls ''consonantal alphabets'' in counterdistinction to alphabets consisting of consonants and vowels, which did not appear until around 750 B.C.E. in Greece (Goody, *Written and Oral,* 40–41).

15. B. L. Ullman, *Ancient Writing and Its Influence,* Medieval Academy Reprints for Teaching 10 (Toronto: University of Toronto Press, 1980 [1932]) 11.

16. Goody, *Written and Oral,* 41.

17. Ibid., 43 and 45.

18. Ibid., 45.

19. This schematic is distilled from Goody's more complex table on the genealogy of the alphabet (ibid., 48, table 2).

20. The Afeg Tablet from the eleventh century, and the Gezer Calendar, probably of the late tenth century, the Davidic period (ibid., 45).

21. Normal K. Gottwald, *The Hebrew Bible* (Philadelphia: Fortress Press, 1985) 567–68.

22. Joseph McIntyre, ''Jeremiah 36 and the Emergence of Scribal Prophecy,'' (unpublished M.A. thesis; Chicago: Catholic Theological Union, 1990) 10.

23. Roland de Vaux, *Ancient Israel,* 2 vols. (New York and Toronto: McGraw-Hill, 1965) 1:49.

24. Namely, the J tradition; see Raymond Brown's chronology of approximate dates of the collection or composition of the works of the Old Testament in the NJBC 66:23.

25. Ong defines ''residual orality'' as ''habits of thought and expression . . . deriving from the dominance of the oral as a medium in a given culture'' (Walter Ong, *Rhetoric, Romance and Technology* [Ithaca, N.Y.: Cornell University Press, 1971] 27–28).

26. The Assyrian monarch Asshurbanipal (668–626 B.C.E.), for example, not only employed numerous scribes and assembled an impressive library, but himself mastered the art of writing (James Mullenberg, ''Baruch the Scribe,'' in *Proclamation and Presence* [Richmond: John Knox Press, 1970] 216.

27. Ibid., 217.

28. McIntyre, ''Scribal Prophecy,'' 11.

29. M. B. Dick, ''Prophetic Poiēsis and the Verbal Icon,'' *Catholic Biblical Quarterly* 46 (1984) 230.

30. R. B. Coote, *Amos among the Prophets: Composition and Theology* (Philadelphia: Fortress Press, 1981).

31. Dick, "Prophetic Poiēsis," 230.

32. McIntyre, "Scribal Prophecy," 4; the following analysis of the role of Jeremiah relies on McIntyre's work.

33. Ibid., 5.

34. McIntyre hypothesizes, "oral cultures seem to be uncertain about how to treat written documents . . . it is evident that Jeremiah 36 is intended to resolve that question. It seems to address the theological issue of preserving a written tradition. . . . I contend that the final form of Jeremiah 36 resolves this situation. It identifies the word of the Lord with the written word of Jeremiah" (ibid., 47–48).

35. Dick, "Prophetic Poiēsis," passim.

36. Ibid., 230–31.

37. Havelock, *The Muse Learns to Write*. In a related comment, Ruth Finnegan notes, "In practice, interaction between oral and written forms is extremely common, and the idea that the use of writing automatically deals a death blow to oral literary forms has nothing to support it" (Ruth Finnegan, *Oral Poetry: Its Nature, Significance and Social Context* [Cambridge: Cambridge University Press, 1977] 160).

38. De Vaux, *Ancient Israel* 1:49.

39. Havelock, *The Muse Learns to Write*, 47.

40. Ibid.; Werner Kelber makes a similar assertion when he suggests that "the objectifying, controlling power of the written medium, while taking the life out of spoken language, can freeze oral forms and preserve them in fossilized profiles" (Werner Kelber, *The Oral and the Written Gospel* [Philadelphia: Fortress Press, 1983] 44).

41. Gerhard Kittel, "ἀκούō," TDNT 1:218.

42. Samuel Terrien, *The Elusive Presence*, Religious Perspectives 26 (San Francisco: Harper & Row, 1978) 69.

43. Kittel, "ἀκούō," TDNT 1:218.

44. Michael Barré, "Amos," NJBC 13:23.

45. Terrien, *Elusive Presence*, 163.

46. See, for example, Joseph Gutmann, *No Graven Images: Studies in Art and the Hebrew Bible* (New York: Ktav, 1970).

47. Richard Clifford, "Exodus," NJBC 3:33.

48. Terrien, *Elusive Presence*, 135.

49. Ibid., 136–38.

50. Some have also suggested that there was an ancient stratum in Israel's history that put emphasis on vision rather than hearing in divine revelation. As J. N. Sanders, for example, notes, "Anciently a prophet was called a 'seer' (1 Sam 9.9). The emphasis on word rather than vision may be connected with the Hebrew rejection of Idolatry and, indeed mistrust of any visual aids to religious faith such as are found in most religions, including Christianity itself" (J. N. Sanders, "Word," IDB 4:869).

51. R. C. Denta, "Ear," IDB 2:1.

52. Thus Wolff concludes, "Just as the auditory reception of the word by the wise man through the ear changes the whole state of the body, so the hearing determines a man's behavior and state of health generally" (Hans Walter Wolff, *Anthropology of the Old Testament*, trans. Margaret Kohl [Philadelphia: Fortress Press, 1974] 76).

53. *Encyclopedic Dictionary of the Bible*, ed. Louis Hartmann (New York: McGraw-Hill, 1963) s.v. "ear" and "heart".

54. Wolff, *Anthropology*, 76.

55. Gerhard von Rad, *Wisdom in Israel*, trans. James Martin (Nashville: Abingdon Press, 1972) 310.

56. Xavier Léon-Dufour, *Dictionary of Biblical Theology*, 2d ed. (New York: Seabury Press, 1973) s.v. "communion."

57. *Encyclopedic Dictionary of the Bible*, s.v. "ear."

58. K. H. Maahs, "Ear," *The International Standard Bible Encyclopedia*, ed. Geoffrey Bromiley, 4 vols. (Grand Rapids: Eerdmans, 1982) 2:2.

59. Kittel, "ákoúō," TDNT 1:218.

60. "According to the Hebraic meaning of the word truth, to listen, to receive the word of God, is not only to lend it an attentive ear but also to open one's heart to it; it is to be put into practice, that is, to obey" (Léon-Dufour, *Dictionary of Biblical Theology*, s.v. "listen").

61. Wolff, *Anthropology*, 77.

62. K. H. Maahs, "Mouth," *The International Standard Bible Encyclopedia*, 2:428.

63. Much of what follows comes from Wolff, *Anthropology*, 77–78.

64. Thorlief Boman, *Hebrew Thought Compared with Greek*, trans. Jules Moreau (Philadelphia: Westminster Press, 1960) 28–31.

65. Ibid., 31.

66. Ibid., 31–35.

67. Ibid., 38–49.

68. Claude Tresmontant, *A Study of Hebrew Thought*, trans. Michael Francis Gibson (New York: Desclee Company, 1960) 125.

69. Boman, *Hebrew Thought*, 49–51. Boman's discussion of the dynamism of Hebrew thought contrasted with Greek thought needs to be read with caution. As will be demonstrated, Greek thought before Plato (d. 347 B.C.E.) was also dynamic; and Hebrew thought after the influence of Alexander the Great demonstrates certain Hellenized influences. Thus, Boman's analysis of what we have called hidden oralisms in the Hebrew Scriptures is especially demonstrative of a type of thinking prominent before the Exile.

70. Evelyn Fox Keller and Christine R. Grontkowski, "The Mind's Eye," in *Discovering Reality*, ed. Sandra Harding and Merrill Hintikka (Dordrecht, Boston, and London: D. Reidel Publishing, 1983) 209.

71. Eric Havelock, *Preface to Plato: A History of the Greek Mind* (Cambridge: Belknap Press of Harvard University Press, 1963) vii. Also Keller and Grontkowski who comment,

So evident was it to him [Plato] that vision enjoys an elevated status over the other senses that he was able merely to assert its preeminence, at least implicitly, without feeling it necessary to argue the point. In his only extensive analysis of the senses per se, he entirely separates the discussion of vision from the discussion of the other four senses [*Timaeus*, 61d–68e]. He describes the creation of the sense of sight in the same context as the creation of soul and intelligence in human beings; all of the other senses are described in the context of the creation of man's material nature. He also says, in Timaeus, that "the first organs they (the gods) fashioned were those that gave us light" [45b]. He comments elsewhere on the intrinsic nobility of this construction, as for example, in Phaedrus, when referring to "the keenest of all the senses" [250d] and in the Republic when he observes: "Have you noticed how extremely lavish the designer of our senses was when he gave us the faculty of sight?" [507c] (Keller and Grontkowski, "The Mind's Eye," 210).

72. Pliny the Elder, for example, speaking about the history of paper, noted how a shortage of paper could completely upset life in the Roman Empire (*Natural History* 13.27.89, ed. H. Rackham in 10 volumes, Loeb Classical Library [Cambridge: Harvard University Press, 1945] 370:153).

73. Paul Achtemeier, "Omne Verbum Sonat: The New Testament and the Oral Environment of Late Western Antiquity," *Journal of Biblical Literature* 109 (1990) 12.

74. Ibid., 15–16. For a corrective to Actemeier, see Frank Gilliard, "More Silent Reading in Antiquity," *Journal of Biblical Literature* 112:4 (1993) 689–96.

75. Jacob Neusner, *The Way of Torah*, 3d ed. (North Scituate, Mass.: Duxbury Press, 1979), 13; also, idem, *The Memorized Torah: The Mnemonic System of the Mishnah* (Chico, Calif.: Scholars Press, 1985).

76. Jacob Neusner, *From Politics to Piety: The Emergence of Pharisaic Judaism* (New York: Ktav, 1979) 11.

77. De Vaux, *Ancient Israel* 1:49.

78. Harold Coward, *Sacred Word and Sacred Text: Scripture in World Religions* (Maryknoll, N.Y.: Orbis Books, 1988) 36.

79. For such a perspective, see Birger Gerhardsson, *The Origins of the Gospel Traditions* (Philadelphia: Fortress Press, 1979).

80. Amos Wilder, *Early Christian Rhetoric: The Language of the Gospel* (Cambridge: Harvard University Press, 1971) 15.

81. Ibid., 13.

82. Coward, *Sacred Word*, 37.

83. Wilder, *Early Christian Rhetoric*, 4.

84. See, for example, E. P. Sanders, *Jesus and Judaism* (Philadelphia: Fortress Press, 1985) 8 and passim.

85. Joachim Jeremias, *The Parables of Jesus*, rev. ed. (New York: Charles Scribner's Sons, 1963); for a summary and critique of Jeremias's position, see Norman Perrin, *Jesus and the Language of the Kingdom* (Philadelphia: Fortress Press, 1976) 91–107.

86. Adela Yarbro Collins, "Eschatology and Apocalypticism," NJBC 81:41.

87. Wilder, *Early Christian Rhetoric*, 14.

88. C. H. Dodd, *The Parables of the Kingdom*, rev. ed. (New York: Scribner's, 1961) 9–10.

89. Wilder, *Early Christian Rhetoric*, 15.

90. David Tracy, *Blessed Rage for Order* (New York: Seabury Press, 1975) 126.

91. Ibid., 130.

92. C. H. Dodd, *The Apostolic Preaching and Its Developments* (Grand Rapids: Baker Book House, 1980) 7–8.

93. Coward, *Sacred Word*, 34.

94. Ernst Fuchs, "Die Sprache im Neuen Testament," in idem, *Zur Frage nach dem historischen Jesus* (Tübingen, 1960) 261, as cited and translated by Wilder, *Early Christian Rhetoric*, 10.

95. Frederick Crowe, *Theology of the Christian Word* (New York: Paulist Press, 1978) 35.

96. Gerhard Friedrich, "kerygma," TDNT 3:716.

97. Kelber, *The Oral and the Written Gospel*, esp. 44–89.

98. Achtemeier, "Omne Verbum Sonat," 19.

99. Wilder, *Early Christian Rhetoric*, 16.

100. Edward Schillebeeckx, *Jesus*, trans. Hubert Hoskins (New York: Vintage Books, 1981) 155.

101. Dominic Crossan, *The Dark Interval* (Niles, Ill.: Argus Publications, 1975) 124.

102. Kelber, *The Oral and Written Gospel*, 58; much of what follows is reliant upon Kelber (ibid., 57–64).

103. Such as alliteration, paranomasia, appositional equivalence, proverbial and aphoristic diction, contrasts and antitheses, synonymous, antithetical, synthetic and tautologic parallelism, etc.; see ibid., 27. For a further discussion of mnemonic devices in oral speech, see Marcel Jousse, *Études de psychologie linguistique: Le style oral rythmique et mnémontechnique chez les verbo-moteurs* (Paris: Gabriel Beauchesne, 1925).

104. Kelber notes that the display of opposites appeals to the imagination and holds the attention as few rhetorical devices do (*The Oral and Written Gospel*, 59).

105. Paul Ricoeur, "Biblical Hermeneutics," *Semeia* 4 (1975) 32; Dominic Crossan calls this an "antitraditional" story element, in *In Parables: The Challenge of the Historical Jesus* (New York: Harper and Row, 1973) 118; Robert Funk calls it the "imaginative shock" in the story, in *Language, Hermeneutic, and the Word of God: The Problem of Language in the New Testament and Contemporary Theology* (New York: Harper and Row, 1966) 193; Wilder calls it the "trait of hyperbole" in these stories, in *Early Christian Rhetoric*, 85.

106. Kelber, *The Oral and the Written Gospel*, 61.

107. Wilhelm Michaelis, "óraō," TDNT 5:361–64.

108. Ibid., 5:348.

109. Wilder, *Early Christian Rhetoric,* 11.

110. 1 Cor 11:23-25; Mark 14:22-24; Matt 26:26-27; Luke 22:19-20; while not a parallel passage, an independent version of Jesus' word of interpretation over the bread can be found in John 6:51c.

111. See Gregory Dix, *The Shape of the Liturgy,* 2d ed. (London: Dacre Press, 1975 [1945]) 48-50.

112. Joachim Jeremias, *The Eucharistic Words of Jesus,* trans. Norman Perrin (Philadelphia: Fortress Press, 1977) 189-96.

113. Ibid., 160-73.

114. Ibid., 105.

115. The current official text of the Latin Rite of the Roman Catholic Church, for example, is a variation on the biblical texts.

116. Goody, *Written and Oral,* 106.

117. Wilder, *Early Christian Rhetoric,* 13.

118. Gino Stefani understands this well in "L'expressione vocale nella liturgia primitiva," *Ephemerides Liturgicae* 84 (1970) esp. 105-6.

FIGURE 1. HEROD'S TEMPLE
Plan of Herod's Temple (after Vincent-Steve as cited in Norman Perrin and
Dennis C. Dulling, *The New Testament: An Introduction*, 2nd ed. (Hartcourt,
Brace, Jovanovich, New York, 1982) p. xx.

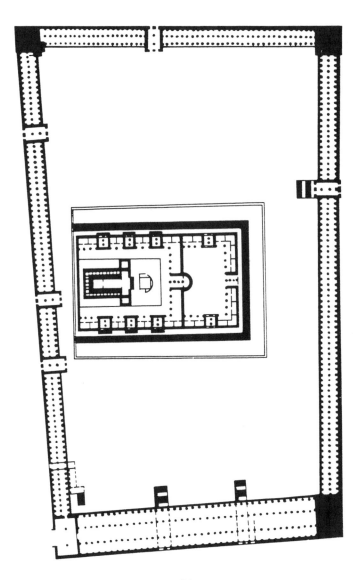

2 The Temple of Herod

The Setting

Following the instruction of his father, King David (d. ca. 962 B.C.E.), Solomon (d. ca. 922 B.C.E.) built the first Temple in Jerusalem (1 Chr 22:6-8). It was a small[1] but sumptuous structure, which took almost seven years to complete (1 Kgs 6:37-38).[2] It soon became the national religious center of Israel, overshadowing every other sanctuary in the country.[3] Destroyed by the invading Babylonians in 587 B.C.E., the Temple was rebuilt according to a more modest plan after the period of captivity, in about 515 B.C.E. (Ezra 5:16; Hag 2:3). Ravaged by time and wars, this structure was in considerable disrepair by the first century B.C.E. Herod the Great (d. 4 B.C.E.) demolished this second Temple and began building a magnificent replacement in about the year 20 B.C.E. This building, completed by 64 C.E., was destroyed in 70 C.E. during the revolt against the Romans.

The new Temple, like the two before it, sat high on a hill overlooking the Kidron valley. The Temple proper in this new complex was about the same size as Solomon's building. It seemed more magnificent, however, because Herod doubled the size of the Temple mount and constructed a far more extensive enclosure wall.[4] Within this impressive enclosed setting was a further series of walls and courtyards. Moving from the outermost to the innermost, these were (1) the Court of the Gentiles, open to all; (2) the Court of the Women, open to all Jews; (3) the Court of Israel,[5] open only to Jewish men; and (4) the Court of the Priests, open only to the priests. The altar for the daily sacrifices stood within the Court of Israel. Sacrifices had once been offered in many different sanctuaries throughout Israel,[6] but the Temple in Jerusalem came to be the only place of sacrifice for the Jews, although Samaritans offered sacrifice on Mount Gerizim.[7] For all practical purposes, the destruction of the Jerusalem Temple in 70 C.E. marked the end of Jewish sacrifice.

Temple Musicians

King David is remembered as having established professional Temple music (1 Chr 15), and having placed Levites in charge (1 Chr 25). The earliest accounts of the Temple (2 Sam 6), however, do not mention professional Temple musicians, which may have been a post-Davidic development.[8] The pre-exilic material in the Hebrew Scriptures gives little evidence for Temple singers. On the other hand, information about other sanctuaries of the same period, both inside and outside Palestine, lead scholars like de Vaux to conclude that the first Temple retained the services of professional musicians.[9]

The role of prophets in the musical life of Israel or the First Temple has never been clear. As Eric Werner notes, they have sometimes been considered priestly Temple singers, or non-priestly singers attached to the Temple, or even independent singers sharply distinct from the musical hierarchy of the official cult.[10] Whatever their role, they were eventually eclipsed by the Levitical musicians. The earliest evidence indicates that Levitical musicians needed to be at least thirty years of age in order to serve in the Temple,[11] although this age limit fluctuated,[12] possibly because of an increased demand for Levites in the service of the Temple.[13] One source indicates that Levites served only until they were fifty years of age (Num 4:3).

According to the Chronicler, 288 musicians were appointed to serve in the Temple (1 Chr 25:7). While this may simply be a mythic number born of the Chronicler's fertile imagination, its historicity—especially for the post-exilic Temple—cannot be completely discounted. The Chronicler notes that priests were divided into twenty-four classes or sections, and that the time of service for each section was determined by casting lots (1 Chr 24:4-18). The Levites, also divided into twenty-four sections, similarly cast lots in order to determine the sequence of their service (1 Chr 25:9-31). Each section of priests and Levites served in the Temple for a week at a time, twice yearly.[14] The Chronicler's calculation of 288 musicians allows for the existence of twenty-four sections, each comprised of 12 musicians. Although one cannot project this number into pre-exilic times, it does reinforce the impression that musicians of the first Temple served in groups of singers and/or instrumentalists rather than as individual precentors.[15] The number of musicians who served in the post-exilic Temple was apparently larger than that of the first Temple.[16]

It is quite possible that 12 was the minimum number of musicians required to accompany sacrifices.[17] The Mishnah puts the minimum number of Levitical musicians at 12.[18] This number is repeated by various authors, but usually as a specific reference to the number of instrumentalists in the Temple.[19] A. Z. Idelsohn further suggests that there was a minimum of 12 singers as well at each Temple service. It is possible, however, that the mishnaic passage which Idelsohn relies upon for this conclusion[20] is not referring to singers alone, but to Levites who sing and accompany themselves on lyres and harps.[21]

While a Levite's position was hereditary, the training for Temple musicianship developed beyond familial tutoring. Late rabbinic sources report that the musical training of a Levitical singer took at least five years of intensive preparation.[22] While this suggests a very sophisticated training process, such is not improbable given the intricate workings of the post-exilic Temple as reported by the Chronicler as well as the developed state of professional musicianship in the royal courts and Temples of the ancient Near East.[23] As members of a professional ''singing guild,''[24] it is quite probable that the post-exilic Levitical singers underwent lengthy training and apprenticeships before assuming any regular musical role in Israel's national worship.

In summary, we can say that Temple musicians served in groups not as individuals; there seems to have been a balance between instruments and voices in the music of the Temple; most of the accompanying instruments were string instruments;[25] the musicians were ordinarily male,[26] adults,[27] well trained, and (at least in post-exilic times) Levites; the number 12 was an idealized quorum of Temple musicians.

Temple Song

It is common to refer to the Psalter as the songbook of the Temple. This phrase is as helpful as it is misleading. There is general agreement today—largely because of the work of Sigmund Mowinckel[28]— that, from their inception, the psalms were intimately related to Israel's cult. This does not mean, however, that all or even most of the psalms were related to Temple worship.[29] Very few of the psalms have specific and identifiable liturgical references that allow them to be linked with any certainty to worship[30] or, more particularly, to worship in the Temple. While the structure and content of some psalms suggests that they were employed in the rituals of the Temple,[31] and the Mishnah remembers that certain others were sung on particular days in the Temple,[32] not all of them were employed there,[33] and other texts besides the psalms were sung in Temple worship.

While it is not possible to identify with certainty these other texts, the Old Testament does offer some clues. As Stuhlmueller notes, ancient Israel undoubtedly possessed collections of sacred melodies that developed at its various shrines as well as various traditional songs that would have been sung at community gatherings.[34] Examples of the latter include the song of Deborah (Judg 5), the blessing of Moses (Deut 33), and the song of Moses (Deut 32). Who is to say that such traditional or community songs were not a part of Temple worship?—especially in the early years of the Temple when the songs of the common people rather than those of the professional musicians may have dominated. The Mishnah gives the impression that the song of Moses (Exod 15:1-18) was employed in Temple worship.[35] Besides these longer songs, various hymnic fragments appear throughout the Old Testament.[36] These might well be remnants of the "new hymns" that the psalmist insists one need sing to the Lord.[37] According to the Mishnah, the daily Temple services also included a prayer service celebrated by the priests.[38] This service would have included the recitation of the Decalogue, the Shema,[39] a series of benedictions, a psalm, and a blessing over the people. While the Mishnah envisions that most of these prayer-elements were chanted by the priests, it is also probable that—to the extent that such a daily service existed—the Levites and even the ordinary Jews in attendance participated. Whatever the exact nature of the divergent texts employed in Temple worship, Werner believes that the psalmist's exhortation to "sing to the Lord a new song" is clear evidence that a change in the musical repertoire was nothing new for the Levites in service of the Temple.[40]

"Song" Forms

Since we do not know much about the texts that were sung in Temple worship, it is difficult to outline with exactitude the accompanying musical forms. However, there are some recognizable structures embedded in existing texts as well as some "stage directions" in the Old Testament that offer hints about the musical forms of Temple song.

Some Temple music undoubtedly included the voices of the people along with those of the musical specialists. Stuhlmueller's analysis of Psalm 44, for example, suggests how individual singers, a choir, and a larger assembly could have joined together in this hymn.[41] Psalm 136, the only Old Testament psalm with a refrain after every colon,[42] offers another instance where amateur voices joining on this refrain might have blended with professional musicians in Temple song. The Mishnah remembers a responsorial form in which the congregation responded to each verse with some brief refrain.[43] In a similar way, the assembly might have punctuated other psalms with cries of "Hallelujah."[44] It appears, therefore, that a variety of forms that divided the music between the professional musicians and the ordinary worshippers were employed in Temple worship.[45] It is also possible that some psalms (or sections of psalms) were divided amongst groups of Levitical singers.[46]

Other psalms or sacred song texts could have been rendered strophically. The existence of strophic forms is suggested by the structure of psalms such as 119. This longest psalm in the Hebrew Scriptures is comprised of 176 lines, grouped in twenty-two stanzas of 8 lines each.[47] The symmetry of the text intimates a similar symmetry in the song structure, that is, a strophic form.

While there is no evidence that this particular psalm was employed in Temple worship, its presence within the Psalter suggests the existence of strophic forms within the tradition of Jewish cultic song. Werner proposes that the form of many longer canticles or psalms "must have been strophic, as without any such repetition . . . it was not possible to keep together the vocal and instrumental ensemble."[48] It is also possible that some psalms or sacred songs were rendered as through-composed works.[49]

Instruments

While there are at least nineteen identifiable terms for musical instruments in the First Testament,[50] not all of these instruments were regularly used in Temple worship. Some, like the *ḥaẓoẓerah* (trumpet), were frequently employed in Temple worship and "the sounding of the trumpet was to be the duty and privilege of the Aaronite priests who exercised it both in war (2 Chr 13:12) and in sacred ceremonies (Num 10:8)."[51] Other instruments, such as the very popular *tof*,[52]—although used to accompany religious ecstasy (1 Sam 10:15) and songs of divine praise (Ps 81:3)—were not played in the

Temple, at least by the time it was populated by professional musicians.[53] In general, one can suggest that instrumental music in the second Temple was limited to trumpet flourishes, a large body of string instruments and a small number (or even single pair) of cymbals.[54] Instruments seems to have played an even more reduced role in the music of the first Temple.[55]

The lack of surety about the number and identity of musical instruments in the First Testament hints at an even greater confusion about the usage of such instruments in Temple worship. Little is known for certain concerning instrumental performance practices in the Temple of any age. Given the types of instruments that probably were played in this worship, it is possible to suggest that instrumental music in the Temple was used either for signalling purposes or to accompany vocal music. The *ḥazozerah*, for example, probably produced a relatively high and shrill sound[56] that was more appropriate for signalling the entrance of ministers or announcing a sacrifice (Num 10:10) than accompanying the human voice. The evidence that these instruments were virtually always used in pairs or even larger groupings[57] as well as the numerous examples from the First Testament and the New Testament underscore this "signalling" usage.[58] There appears to have been no independent instrumental music.

The instruments used to accompany the Levitical song were most probably string instruments (Amos 5:23), possibly percussion and very occasionally a woodwind.[59] Werner suggests that "the instrumental accompaniment was probably heterophonic, i.e., it reproduced the vocal line in an instrumental unison with slight melismatic deviations."[60]

Summary on Temple Music

The paucity of clear information about the music of the Temple allows only the most general of conclusions.[61] Although probably not present at its inception, professional musicians soon came to dominate the Temple's music. In the relatively expansive musical vocabulary of the Jews, the terms for vocal music far outnumber the purely instrumental ones.[62] One can surmise that vocal rather than instrumental music similarly dominated. Instruments, apart from their signalling role, probably served to support the vocal music. While there may have been some instances of solo performance, it was not the norm and choral music seem to have dominated.[63] The singing of religious texts appears to have followed the offering of sacrifices (2 Chr 29:20-30) and trumpet blasts often accompanied the sacrifices (Num 10:10). Later rabbinic literature[64] as well as the writings of Josephus (d. ca. 100 C.E.)[65] further note the connection between instrumental music and sacrifice in the Temple. In a later period the Talmud taught that the lack of singing invalidated the sacrificial act.[66] This limited information suggests to Werner that all music of the Temple, regardless of the period, was nothing but an accessory to its sacrificial ritual.[67] In this sacrificial context, the professional Levitical musicians dominated the musical landscape.[68]

The Influence of Temple Music on Christian Practice

Jesus' entire life was framed by Temple experiences. Eight days after his birth he was presented for circumcision in the Temple (Luke 2:21) and while he was on the cross the Temple veil was rent in two (Matt 27:51). Jesus is remembered as having traveled to the Temple as a child, especially during the great pilgrim feasts such as Passover (Luke 2:41). As an adult he frequented the Temple during his public ministry. There he prayed, taught, cured the sick, and challenged contemporary religious practice (Matt 21:12, 14). After his resurrection, the disciples continued to worship and evangelize in the Temple precincts (Acts 2:46; 3:1-11; 21:26). Although the Temple was a place of increasing tension for the disciples as they distinguished themselves from other Jews, the early Jewish Christians never completely rejected the Temple or its worship. On the other hand, Temple sacrifice, which was essential to Jewish cult, became increasingly peripheral for emerging Christianity, especially with the mission to the Gentiles. The destruction of the Temple in 70 C.E. was undoubtedly a great blow to the Jewish Christian community, although its effect on the ritual practices of Jewish Christians is less clear.

Temple music exerted little direct influence on the music of emerging Christianity. Professional guilds of musicians, instrumental accompaniment, and music designed for sacrifice were foreign to the early Christian experience.[69] On the other hand, Temple practice reveals that music played a central role at the very heart of the Jewish cult. Thus, the music of the Temple, as part of the sonic landscape of Jewish cult, contributed to the awareness in emerging Christianity that worship was, by its very nature, a lyric event.

CHAPTER TWO NOTES

1. It measured approximately 105 feet long and 30 feet wide (John Castelot, "Religious Institutions of Israel," NJBC 76:43).

2. On the architecture of Solomon's Temple, see Jean Ouelette, "The Solomonic Debîr according to the Hebrew Text of 1 Kings 6," *Journal of Biblical Literature* 89 (1970) 338–43.

3. E.g., Beersheba (Gen 26:25), Bethel (Gen 12:8), Dan (Judg 18:29-31), Gilgal (Josh 4:19-20), Mamre (Gen 13:18), Mizpah (Judg 20:1), Ophrah (Judg 6:11f.), Shechem (Gen 12:6-7), and Shiloh (Josh 18:1).

4. Robert North, "Biblical Archaeology," NJBC 74:138.

5. According to the Mishnah, Temple musicians stood on a platform that divided the Court of Priests from the Court of Israel (*Middoth* 2.6). Bathja Bayer's comments about the value of the Mishnah in reconstructing Temple worship are worth repeating: "Much of the mishnaic narrative concerning music in the Temple service is based on eyewitness memories. The information is often very precise, such as the description of the daily morning sacrifice in Mishnah Tamid and the numbers of instruments in the Temple orchestra in Mishnah Arakhin. The figure of the Temple Musician appears much more clearly" (Bathja Bayer, "Music," EJ 12:566).

6. See n. 3 above; sacrifices were also offered at Beersheba (Gen 46:1), Bethshemesh (1 Sam 6:15), Hebron (2 Sam 15:12), Shiloh (1 Sam 1:4), etc.

7. This Temple seems to date, according to archaeological evidence, from early in the Greek Era (333–63 B.C.E.). See, for example, Robert Bull, "The Excavation of Tell er-Ras on Mt. Gerizim," *Biblical Archaeologist* 31 (1968) 58–72.

8. This discrepancy serves as a reminder that, although Chronicles describes practices of the first Temple, the post-exilic composition of Chronicles raises serious questions about the accuracy of much of this information. See the summary by Robert North, "The Chronicler," NJBC 23:4 and 6.

9. De Vaux, *Ancient Israel* 2:382; de Vaux also surmises that, since singers "returned" from exile (Neh 7:44), these offices must have existed before the Exile, although "in those days they would not have been Levites" (ibid.).

10. Eric Werner, "Jewish Music: Liturgical," NGDMM 9:617.

11. 1 Chronicles 23:3; also Numbers 4:3 and 2 Chronicles 31:17.

12. In Numbers 8:24 the age requirement for Levitical service is twenty-five, and in Ezra 3:8 and 1 Chronicles 23:27 it is lowered to twenty years of age.

13. Robert North, " 'Kittim' war or 'Sectaries' Liturgy?" *Biblica* 39 (1958) 90.

14. "Forty-eight weeks of the year were thus distributed between twenty-four divisions; the remaining weeks being festival weeks . . . during which all Israel made pilgrimage to Jerusalem" (Philip Birnbaum, *Encyclopedia of Jewish Concepts* [New York: Sanhedrin Press, 1979] s.v. "Ma'amadoth".

15. This is made all the more believable when one reckons with the demands of music making in an outdoor setting, as well as the need for this music to accompany (i.e., cover the sounds of) animal sacrifices.

16. De Vaux, *Ancient Israel* 2:392.

17. I say "minimum" because, even if a division of twelve Levites assumed responsibility for Temple music for one week every six months, it is unlikely that they would be sufficiently familiar with the Temple rituals and procedures to execute their duties without the help (and musical support?) of the regular Temple staff, such as the director of music noted in the Mishnah (*Shekalim* 5.1). Joachim Jeremias suggests that there were two permanent Levite musicians in the Temple who oversaw the music and coordinated the groups of Levites taking their turn in service to the Temple (Joachim Jeremias, *Jerusalem in the Time of Jesus* [Philadelphia: Fortress Press, 1969] 173 and 208).

18. *Arakhin* 2.6.

19. A. Z. Idelsohn, for example, states, "the total minimum number required for the orchestra was twelve instruments (i.e., a minimum of two lyres: [*nēbel*], a minimum of nine harps: [*kinnôr*], and one cymbal), to which two ḥālīl [flutes] were added on twelve festal days during the year" (A. Z. Idelsohn, *Jewish Music* [New York: Schocken Books, 1967 (1929)] 17). Werner also notes that the Temple's orchestra consisted of never less than twelve and rarely more than thirty-six instruments (Eric Werner, *The Sacred Bridge,* vol. 2 [New York: Ktav, 1984] 3). Jeremias cites *Arakhin* 2.6 as evidence that there must be no less than twelve singers serving in the Temple at one time (Jeremias, *Jerusalem in the Time of Jesus,* 208 n. 199).

It is possible to calculate a requirement of twelve instrumentalists in the Mishnah from a passage in *Arakhin* 2.5, which states, "There were never less than two trumpets, and their number could be increased without end; there were never less than nine lyres, and their number could be increased without end; but of cymbals there was but one." However, this passage does not reconcile with an earlier section in the same tractate which notes, "They played on never less than two harps or more than six" (*Arakhin* 2.3). Werner does comment that "the trumpets were never mixed with the rest of the orchestra—being used for signals exclusively" (Werner, *Sacred Bridge* 2:3). Substituting the two "harps" for the two "trumpets" would render the number twelve and seem to reconcile these two passages.

20. *Arakhin* 2.6.

21. This interpretation is bolstered by the continuation of that passage which allows for [male] children to join in the music making. The children "did not join in the singing with harp and lyre, but with the mouth alone." The implication is that the adults, on the other hand, join in the singing with lyre and harp, that is, accompany themselves on instruments.

22. *B. Hullin* 24a.

23. Alfred Sendry's suggestion that ancient Israel knew an "Academy of Music . . . in which hundreds of students were continuously trained for a professional career" is an extreme view and unsupported by the evidence (Alfred Sendry, *Music in the Social and Religious Life of Antiquity* [Rutherford, Madison, and Teaneck: Fairleigh Dickinson University Press, 1974] 103–4).

24. H. H. Rowley, *Worship in Ancient Israel: Its Forms and Meaning* (London: SPCK, 1967) 205.

25. "A small male choir (occasionally heightened by boys' descants) accompanied only by the plucked strings of lyres and harps; cymbals, trumpets and horns sounded only between the musical sections marked in the Psalm text with the word selah. This reserved character of hebrew Temple music contrasts sharply with the drumming, rattling, and ecstatic clamour heard in most of the heathen cult rituals" (Hanoch Avenary, *The New Oxford Companion to Music*, ed. Denis Arnold, 2 vols. [Oxford and New York: Oxford University Press, 1983] s.v. "Jewish Music").

26. While women definitely assumed musical roles in the courts of the ancient monarchy, and might have contributed to the music making of the early Temple, their participation "in the Temple choir is nowhere traceable" (Idelsohn, *Jewish Music,* 16). Sendry offers a different perspective: "There is no doubt that women, too, participated in the Levitical music, at least in the early period" (Sendry, *Music in the Social and Religious Life of Antiquity,* 104).

27. Boys did join on certain occasions.

28. For example, see Sigmund Mowinckel, *The Psalms in Israel's Worship,* 2 vols., trans. D. R. Ap-Thomas (Oxford: Basil Blackwell, 1962).

29. "It is possible that fewer psalms were composed directly for the Temple liturgy than we often suppose to have been the case. The Temple, moreover, exercised less direction in the formation of the psalter than we are inclined to think" (Carroll Stuhlmueller, *Psalms: A Biblical-Theological Commentary,* 2 vols., Old Testament Message 21–22 [Wilmington: Michael Glazier, 1983] 1:47).

30. Psalm 81, for example, seems clearly related to the feast of Tabernacles.

31. Psalm 15, for example, may have been employed as part of an entrance liturgy in the Temple; Psalm 24 may have accompanied a liturgical procession to the Temple.

32. "This was the singing which the Levites used to sing in the Temple. On the first day they sang 'The earth is the Lord's and all that therein is, the round world and they that dwell therein' [Ps 24]; on the second day they sang 'Great is the Lord and highly to be praised in the city of our God, even upon his holy hill' [Ps 48]; on the third day they sang 'God standeth in the congregation of God, he is a judge among the gods' [Ps 82]; on the fourth day they sang 'O Lord God to whom vengeance belongeth, thou God to whom vengeance belongeth show thyself' [Ps 94]; on the fifth day they sang 'Sing we merrily unto God our strength, make a cheerful noise unto the God of Jacob' [Ps 81]; on the sixth day they sang 'The Lord is king, and hath put on glorious apparel' [Ps 93]. On the Sabbath they sang 'A Psalm: A Song for the Sabbath Day' [Ps 92]" (*Tamid* 7.4).

33. Mowinckel's analysis suggests that some private psalms were "recited in small groups in ancient Israel, outside of Temple worship" (Mowinckel, *The Psalms in Israel's Worship,* 2:88).

34. Stuhlmueller, *Psalms,* 1:44-45.

35. *Sotah* 5.4.

36. For example Jeremiah 20:13 or Amos 4:13; 5:8-9; 9:5-6 as noted in Stuhlmueller, *Psalms*, 1:47.

37. Psalms 33:3; 96:1; 98:1; 144:9; 149:1.

38. *Tamid* 5.1; see the discussion of this service in Allan Bouley, *From Freedom to Formula*, The Catholic University of America Studies in Christian Antiquity 21 (Washington, D.C.: The Catholic University of America Press, 1981) 7–13.

39. Composed of three biblical texts: Deut 6:4-9; 11:13-21; Num 15:37-41.

40. Eric Werner, "Music," IDB 3:463a.

41.   Vv. 1–8: Hymnic Introduction

vv. 1:2:	Call to praise, sung by everyone
v. 3:	Motivation, sung by large choir
v. 4:	sung by individual cantor or special choir
v. 6:	sung by individual cantor or special choir
v. 8:	choral refrain by everyone

Vv. 9–16: Community Lament

v. 15:	sung by individual cantor or choir	
vv. 17–22	Reflection, sung by different choirs who	
	vv. 17–19	speak to God
	vv. 20–21	speak about God
	v. 22	speak to God.

Stuhlmueller, *Psalms*, 1:234.

42. John S. Kselman and Michael Barré, "Psalms," NJBC 34:153. For a further discussion of the evidence of "refrains" in the psalms, see Alfred Sendry, *Music in Ancient Israel* (New York: Philosophical Library, 1969) 173–74.

43. Speaking of the song in Exodus, the Mishnah comments, "It teaches us that Israel made answer to everything after Moses, like as when they recited the Hallel" (*Sotah* 5:4; also *Sukkah* 3.10).

44. For example, Psalms 146–50.

45. In discussing the origins of the various forms of Jewish psalmody, Hanoch Avenary notes, "The various kinds of Jewish psalmody arose from one formal principle: the confrontation of soloist and choir (responsorial psalmody)" (Hanoch Avenary, "Formal Structure of Psalms and Canticles in Early Jewish and Christian Chant," *Musica Disciplina* 7 [1953] 3).

46. See, for example, the alternating structure in Psalm 103:20-22; such alternation, as Gelineau points out, is rooted in a parallelism endemic to Semitic poetry, in which the literary form of certain psalms is an "invitation to dialogue" (Joseph Gelineau, "Les formes de la psalmodie chrétienne," *La Maison-Dieu* 33 [1953] 163).

47. The organizational principle here is the Hebrew alphabet of twenty-two letters; each stanza (and every line of that stanza) begins with a different letter of the Hebrew alphabet, so that all twenty-two letters have a complete stanza, in alphabetical order (Stuhlmueller, *Psalms*, 2:152).

48. Werner, "Music," IDB 3:463.

49. A psalm such as 117, for example, is brief enough to have had its own melody, easily memorized, and tied only to this text.

50. While various scholars calculate these numbers differently, and offer various descriptions of such instruments, we produce here the relatively comprehensive yet conservatively described list of Bayer, plus a single biblical reference for each instrument: (1) *asor* (Ps 33:2), perhaps a small *nevel* with only ten strings; (2) *ḥalil* (1 Sam 10:5), double-pipe wind instrument; (3) *ḥaẓoẓerah* (Hos 5:8), trumpet, made of precious metal, generally silver; (4) *kaitros/katros* (Dan 3:5), Aramaic term for the Greek string instrument known as the *kithera*; (5) *keren* (Josh 6:5), probably another term for the *shofar*; (6) *kinnor* (Ps 150:3), string instrument of the lyre family, constituted by a body, two arms, and a yoke; (7) *maśhrokita* (Dan 3:5), Aramaic term for a whistling or piping instrument employed in the court of the Babylonian king; (8) *mena'ane'im* (2 Sam 6:5), possibly a pottery rattle; (9) *meẓiltayim* (Ezra 3:10), *ẓilẓalim* (2 Sam 6:5), *meẓillot* (Zech 14:20), the first two forms probably stand for cymbals, while the third "instrument" probably consisted of metal ball-jingles; (10) *minnim* (Ps 150:5), an unclear term, presumably a string instrument, perhaps a lute; (11) *nevel* (Ps 150:3), a type of lyre, larger than the *kinnor* and, therefore, of deeper tone; (12) *pa'amon* (Exod 28:33), bells (originally metal platelets?) attached to the tunic of the high priest; (13) *pesanterin* (Dan 3:5), Aramaic term for the Greek string instrument known as the *psalterion*; (14) *sabbekha* (Dan 3:5), Aramaic term for the Greek (string?) instrument known as the *sambyke*; (15) *shalishim* (1 Sam 18:6), possibly cymbals or struck metal bowls; (16) *shofar* (1 Chr 15:28) horn of the ram or a wild ovine, probably identical with the *keren*; (17) *sumponyah* (Dan 3:5), although sometimes identified as a "bagpipe" (e.g., NAB), this Aramaic term is probably not a reference to a specific instrument but parallels the Greek *symphoneia*, which in itself means only "the sounding together"; (18) *tof* (2 Sam 6:5), a shallow round-frame drum; and (19) *ugav* Gen 4:21), unclear but very probably not the wind instrument that medieval exegesis suggested, it could have been a harp (Bathja Bayer, "Music," EJ 12:560).

51. D. A. Foxvog and A. D. Kilmer, "Music," *International Standard Bible Encyclopedia*, ed. Geoffrey Bromiley, 4 vols. (Grand Rapids: Eerdmans, 1986) 3:439.

52. It is mentioned seventeen times in the Old Testament; see Werner, "Music," IDB 3:474.

53. In the case of the *tof*, this is possibly because it was played mainly by women (e.g., Exod 15:20; Judg 11:35, 1 Sam 18:6; etc.) who assumed no role among the Temple's professional musicians.

54. Bayer, "Music," EJ 12:560; as to the specific instruments employed in the Temple, the Mishnah mentions the *kinnor, nevel, ḥaẓoẓerah, meẓiltayim, ẓilẓalis* the *shofar* and the *ḥalil* (*Arakhin* 2.3, 5).

55. Bayer calls it "minimal" (ibid.).

56. See Werner, "Musical Instruments," IDB 3:472.

57. "In twenty-eight of its twenty-nine occurrences, *ḥaẓoẓerah* appears in the plural, and it can be assumed that the trumpets were sounded in pairs or in

larger ensembles, both to magnify their effect and to fulfill the command of Num 10.2" (Foxvog and Kilmer, "Music," 3:440).

58. E.g., Num 10:2; 1 Chr 15:24; Rev 8–11.

59. Werner suggests that, especially for solo singing, "a highly differentiated accompaniment without a blending of the various timbres is desired, and for choral singing (with woodwind instruments, harps or lyres and percussion), sharp, high-pitched, rhythmically accentuated sounds" (Werner, "Jewish Music," NGDMM 9:620).

60. Werner, "Instrumental Music," IDB 3:463.

61. The sound of this music is even more problematic that its structure, texts, or the identity of the musicians. In this pre-notation period there was no accurate way to notate musical sound and preserve it for posterity. There have been many attempts to reconstruct the various modes and melodies that served as the building blocks for ancient Jewish music (for example, Idelsohn in *Jewish Music*). The speculative and technical nature of such reconstructions, however, do not recommend that we pursue the topic here.

62. Werner, "Music," IDB 3:460.

63. Werner, "Jewish Music," NGDMM 9:622.

64. The Mishnah and Talmud, for example, usually identify various musical activities by referring to specific sacrifices (*Arakhin* 2.3–6; *B. Arakhin* 11a; *Tamid* 7.3–4; *B. Ta'anith* 27a).

65. Josephus, *Antiquities of the Jews* 7.12.3; also *Jewish War* 11.9.15; 15.8.1; 3.777; 9.4.2.

66. *B. Arakin* 11a.

67. Werner, "Music," IDB 3:459.

68. In one of his last published works, Werner went even further in drawing the connection between the institution of sacrifice, hierarchy, and professional or "art" music (Werner, *Sacred Bridge*, 2:149ff.).

69. It is somewhat ironic that these musical elements re-emerged in Christianity after it had wed itself to the empire in the fourth century.

3 Synagogues of the First Century C.E.

The Setting

Unlike the Temple, the origins of the Jewish synagogue are yet in doubt. As Joseph Gutmann summarizes,[1] there are three major theories current among scholars to explain the origins of the synagogue. Most scholars subscribe to the theory that the synagogue emerged during the Babylonian Exile. A second group favors the Deuteronomic origin of the synagogue. Finally, a small group holds for a Hellenistic beginning of the synagogue in third-century B.C.E. Egypt. According to Gutmann, however, the bases for all three theories are a faulty semantic analysis and inadequate historical conceptualization.[2] Firm literary evidence for the existence of the synagogue is extant only from the first century C.E., specifically in the writings of Philo (d. ca. 50 C.E.),[3] Josephus (d. ca. 100 C.E.),[4] and the New Testament.[5] Archaeological evidence from the first century is neither as plentiful nor as firm.[6] Such lack of evidence combined with other historical and theological factors leads Gutmann to suggest that the synagogue arose only in the second century B.C.E.[7]

The reevaluation of the origins of the synagogue, especially in view of extant archaeological evidence, has led scholars to reevaluate the various theories about the architecture of primitive synagogues. With increasing frequency, the dominant ''evolutionary'' theory—that there was an early Galilean prototype synagogue from which other synagogue types evolved in clear cut, chronological stages—is giving way to the more complex theory of the coexistence of many types of synagogues in the early period.[8] Such a shift allows one to offer few generalizations about the physical setting of the first-century C.E. synagogue.

Andrew Seager suggests that the earliest synagogues were simple structures without much elaboration in their plan, whereas later synagogues tended to be more highly differentiated, possibly reflecting an evolving interest in ritual and liturgy.[6] For example, the Torah was given an increasingly prominent setting as Scripture became more important to the community. In some cases a fixed repository for the Torah was a later addition to an already existing and functioning synagogue. While of varying sizes and shapes, early synagogues did tend to be relatively open structures. Some synagogues were orientated toward Jerusalem, and some were not.

Synagogue "Musicians"

It is especially when speaking about the synagogue that our modern distinction between music and public speech blurs.[10] The presence of choirs and orchestras in the Temple allows us to speak with some clarity about its "music" and, by consequence, to speak about Temple musicians. Such is more difficult, however, when discussing the synagogue. As a place where prayers were offered and the word was proclaimed, the synagogue was devoid of instrumental or choral music properly speaking. The performance of synagogal, word-centered worship continuously migrated back and forth between what we might call speech and song.[11] While it was virtually always lyrical, in the broad sense of that term,[12] the modern hearer (especially from Western cultures) might not always classify it as musical.[13] This musical ambiguity is underscored by the absence of identifiable musicians in the synagogue for the first centuries of its existence.

As I have suggested before,[14] the absence of an identifiable musician or even fixed prayer leader in the synagogue is wed to an approach to prayer leadership that was decidedly more "democratic" than that found in the Temple.[15] As Idelsohn notes, "In Judaism the idea became prevalent, through the influence of the prophets, that God is near to everybody, and that everybody is worthy of approaching [God]. The relationship between God and Israel, as between [parent] and children, entitled everyone to pray to God without priestly mediation."[16] Joseph Heinemann further asserts that the rise of statutory prayer in the period of the second Temple heralds the "democratization of the divine worship" with a new form of worship "to be performed by each individual, by the entire community of worshippers, wherever they may be."[17] This perspective had a marked influence on the emerging synagogue which was devoid of a professional priesthood.

Because of the unique Jewish perspective on prayer leadership, the execution of the synagogue service was not relegated to an ordained or permanent clergy,[18] and through talmudic and early gaonic times, volunteers functioned as leaders of the service.[19] Such a volunteer was already in the oldest sources called *sheliach tsibbur* (literally "the emissary of the people").[20] These volunteers were sometimes chosen by the elder of the synagogue—the *rosh ha-knesset* or *archisynagogos*—a kind of superintendent who was responsible for overseeing the worship and maintaining order.[21] That the *sheliach tsibbur* could be any member of the congregation is demonstrated by the fact that even women were sometimes selected to mediate in the name of the community.[22] While it is true that standards for selecting the *sheliach tsibbur* emerged by the end of the second century C.E.[23]—and that, with increasing frequency, vocal ability became a determining factor in selecting the honorary precentor[24]—there is no such evidence from the first century C.E. Prayer leadership in the synagogues of that era was not conceived first and foremost as a musical role, and there was no separate or distinctive musician.[25]

Synagogue "Song"

While Temple worship revolved around sacrifice, synagogue services centered on the recitation of various texts. Establishing the various texts or kinds of texts employed in first-century synagogues will enable us to explore something of their lyricism and their lyrical forms.

The Statutory Prayers

In his classic study on the history of Jewish prayer, Heinemann asserts that the institution of fixed, communal prayer constitutes a "radical innovation of the Second Temple period."[26] Considered on a par with the sacrificial cult of the Temple, such obligatory and fixed prayer was understood as a legitimate form of divine worship, through which Israel fulfilled its daily communal obligations to the Lord.[27] Such prayers, oral at their root, were improvised from their inception. Eventually a common repertoire of frequently employed idioms and fixed formulae began to define them; in general, they

FIGURE 2. SYNAGOGUE AT SARDIS

Synagogue at Sardis, originally built as a Roman basilica (first century C.E.). In the foreground is the apse with three rows of benches for the elders of the community. Beyond the apse is the marble table, probably used for the reading of Torah. Toward the back of the hall are the bases of four pillars, which may have supported the reader's desk. At the far end are three entrances with shrines between them, which may have been used for storing the Torah scrolls. Text and illustration after Geoffrey Wigoder, *the Story of the Synagogue* (Harper & Row, San Francisco, 1986) pp. 32–33.

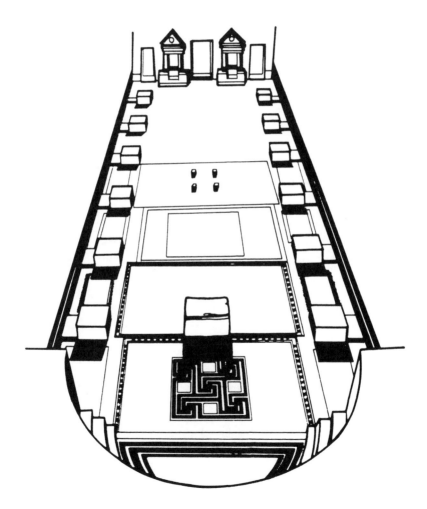

could be considered free-style.[28] The oldest such prayer is the Shema,[29] which is really more of a profession of faith than a prayer. The Shema has traditionally been surrounded by a series of benedictions.[30] While it is not possible to establish with any certainty when these prayers appeared, the Mishnah already notes their existence, and does so in such a way as to suggest that the Shema and "its benedictions" were a well-established unit.[31] It does not appear, however, that the Decalogue, which was linked to the Shema in the Temple liturgy, was ever a standard part of the synagogue liturgy.[32] Another statutory prayer is the eighteen benedictions or *amidah*, which antedated the destruction of Herod's Temple "by a considerable period of time."[33] These two prayer elements, at least, were central to the synagogue services of the first century C.E.[34]

Readings

Publicly reading from both the Law (Torah) and the Prophets (Haftarah) was an ancient synagogue practice.[35] The Lukan passage describing Jesus' reading from the prophet Isaiah in the synagogue at Nazareth underscores the established nature of such reading by reporting a series of well-choreographed ritual actions and procedures surrounding it.[36] Other New Testament passages are explicit about the custom of publicly reading the prophets and the Torah in the synagogue.[37] It became customary—probably during the centuries preceding the destruction of the Temple—to follow the readings from the Law and the Prophets with a series of benedictions.[38] By the time of the Mishnah, the process of enumerating the number of readers and designating particular pericopes for each Sabbath and festival had already begun.[39] This process of standardization, however, did not occur in all places during the Mishnaic period.[40]

Psalmody

It is often suggested that psalmody played a central role in synagogue worship at the dawn of Christianity.[41] This is not, however, demonstrable from the earliest sources.[12] As Werner points out, for example, the Mishnah and Talmud are strangely silent about the commonly accepted linkage between scripture readings and psalmic responses.[43] Positing the existence of scripture readings in the first-century C.E. synagogue service, therefore, does not prove the presence of psalmody—except, perhaps, as "parts of the Holy Scripture, of the authorized and inspired canon, for reading, just like the other biblical books, which were read in the synagogues as holy words of God."[44] Beginning certain services with the recitation of psalms[45] is also a late development, unattested to in the earliest data. While it is true that the recitation of certain psalms as part of the morning service comes from at least the second century of the common era, this was apparently an optional custom.[46] For his part, Heinemann gives no attention to psalmody per se in his discussion of statutory elements of synagogue worship.[47] While the spirit of prayer embodied in the psalms may have influenced synagogal prayer in the first century c.e.—suggested by the incorporation of various psalm phrases into the standard benedictions, and even the composition of new psalm-like pieces for common worship[48]—it is questionable whether psalms were ordinarily sung in first-century synagogue worship. Rather, as Johann Maier summarizes, the psalms were valued first of all as biblical texts, not as a collection of songs.[49]

"Song" Forms

As previously noted, there is more surety about the form of ancient Jewish prayer forms than there is about their melodic or rhythmic structure. We will, therefore, concentrate on the former and offer a few reflections on the latter.

The Statutory Prayers

The creedal nature of the Shema suggests that every Jew knew this profession of faith by heart—a suggestion bolstered by the pointed biblical injunction to "drill" these words into every child and to "mark" body and home with them.[50] It is possible, therefore, that at an early stage the Shema could have been chanted in unison by the whole assembly during the service. Evidence from the earliest stage of the codification of the synagogue service, however, suggests that a *sheliach tsibbur* led the congregation in the recitation of the Shema, reciting the confession and its benedictions line by line from his or her place, while the congregation repeated and completed each verse in course.[51] More plausible, however, is Reuven Kimelman's suggestion that a more complete antiphonal form was employed, that is, the congregation did not repeat any section intoned by the reader,[52] but simply completed the verse.[53] Any of these styles, however, would have required relatively simple musical settings for these congregational chants.

While the Mishnah does acknowledge that it was possible—even necessary—to pray the *amidah* every day, it simultaneously underscores the demanding nature of this prayer,[54] not only because of its length, but also because of the fluid state of its text. As Hoffman notes,

> though the prayer . . . became a staple daily liturgical portion with specifically stipulated petitionary themes officially arranged in orderly sequence, there still remained great differences among the *tannaim*[55] as to the requisite number of blessings and the wording thereof. It may be that blessing topics were settled upon, and even some sample eulogies which seemed more representative of the prayer's basic intent than others. Yet even here it is hard to imagine a final and absolute crystallization until after the promulgation of the Mishnah.[56]

The common recitation of the *amidah* by the whole assembly would have been virtually impossible. Rather, we may conclude that the *amidah* was ordinarily led by the *sheliach tsibbur*,[57] who improvised this series of benedictions according to increasingly standardized formulae; the assembly may have added some phrases of blessing or affirmation at least at the end of the prayer.[58]

Since these prayers were led by ordinary people—and sometimes echoed by the entire congregation—the settings were, by necessity, simple. At the same time, the fluid nature of the evolving prayer texts dictated that such prayer settings were "of a plastic and variable nature in order to be fitted to longer or shorter phrases of the prose texts without difficulty."[59] In response to this need there developed certain "prayer modes,"[60] probably based on already existent modes employed for chanting biblical texts.[61] As to the sound of these modes, Avenary summarizes, "Although it is impossible to ascribe individual tunes heard today to the early synagogue with any degree of certainty, it is legitimate to speak of the principle of chanting according to a nusah."[62]

The Readings

Specific evidence for chanting the readings from Torah and the prophets in the synagogue is imbedded in the Babylonian Talmud. This sixth-century source "remembers" teachings about chanted biblical texts from as early as the second century C.E. For example, it reports that Rabbi Akiba (d. ca. 135 C.E.) stressed the necessity of daily chanting the Scriptures when studying them.[63] It further reports that Rav (d. ca. 250 C.E.) interpreted a section of the Book of Nehemiah (8:8) as a reference to "punctuation by means of melodic cadences."[64] The most celebrated passage of the Talmud about chanting the readings is ascribed to Johanan: "He who reads the Torah without chant . . . of him can it be said as it is written, 'the laws that I gave you were not good' (Ezek 20:25)."[65] Werner assesses this last saying with the comment, "to recite scripture without chant was considered a minor sacrilege."[66]

It is not possible to establish with certainty when this tradition of chanting the Scriptures at synagogue services began. Given the previously elaborated profile about the acoustic environment of the ancient world in general, and ancient Judaism in particular, it would be difficult to imagine any public reading in the synagogue that was not fundamentally lyrical.[67] At the beginning of this tradition, it could have simply involved a heightened declamation of the text, or the employment of simple musical cadences which clarified the structure of each biblical sentence.[68] Eventually there seem to have developed distinctive modes or formulae for the chanting of various types of scripture, like the Law and the Prophets.[69] As the reading of the Torah and the Prophets became more central to the synagogue service[70]—especially after the destruction of the Temple—it became increasingly important to regulate the musical formulae and the use of such formulae when chanting the Scriptures. As Avenary explains,

> Although the text of the Hebrew Bible was fixed long since, every sequence of words could become meaningful only by the correct grouping of the words and a clear interrelation of clauses and subclauses. The division of a verse could become a matter of interpretation, or even ideology, and raise debates with dissenting sects or a foreign creed. It was no wonder that in epochs of insecurity a need was felt to make the accepted infrastructure of biblical verses in an indisputable way—in writing.[71]

That "indisputable way" was the introduction of accents (te'amin) into the written text.[72] Sometimes called "ekphonetic notation,"[73] these accents began to appear in the sixth century.[74] The most important set of these accents was developed by a group of scholars living in the ancient city of Tiberias sometime before the end of the ninth century. This Tiberian system of notation—which, according to tradition, was invented by the family of Ben Asher—was imposed upon the whole of Jewry and is still in use.[75] While some scholars maintain that the Tiberian system was purely syntactical rather than musical,[76] others believe that this system of accents reflects a musical system that developed before the emergence of Christianity and can be reconstructed today.[77] Most scholars do not believe, however, that a clear deciphering of the Tiberian system is possible, or that one can demonstrate an indisputable link between it and the most ancient traditions of biblical cantillation. A series of studies comparing current musical practice with transcriptions made since 1518[78] do suggest, however, that the continuity between ancient and modern synagogue musical practice—passed on through oral tradition—is quite strong.[79]

The benedictions that followed the readings from the Law and the Prophets were likely chanted according to the previously discussed "prayer modes"—improvised according to accepted patterns by the *sheliach tsibbur*, with the assembly adding some phrases of blessing or affirmation at least at the end of the prayer.

Instruments

While the Temple was a place of instrumental music, the synagogue was not. Even before the destruction of the Temple in 70 C.E. there is little evidence to suggest that any instruments—possibly with the exception of the *shofar*—were ever used in the synagogue. After 70 C.E. only the *shofar* was employed in synagogue worship.[80] As to the abandonment of all other instrumental music in the synagogue, Werner offers this assessment:

> At the destruction of the Temple all instrumental music apart from that of the shofar was excluded from worship, partly because of the hostility of the Pharisees to such music, partly because of the deep mourning for the Temple and the land, and the disappearance of the levitical functions, including the provision of music for the sanctuary. . . . With the destruction of the Temple the hour of the rabbis struck. During the next five or six centuries they patched up a legal framework for the general prohibition of all instrumental music, from various and not always convincing arguments. . . . This exclusion of instruments from Jewish worship remained in force generally for many centuries; only at the loss of political power by the rabbis in

the 19th century Emancipation did instrumental music once again appear in the (liberal) synagogue, and the exclusion still remains in force where, as in modern Israel, orthodox rabbis retain some power.[81]

Summary on Synagogue Music

While there is much about ancient synagogal music that we do not know, there are a number of basic assertions that we can make about it, especially as contrasted with the music of the ancient Temple. While the music of the Temple was predominantly vocal, the music of the synagogue was exclusively vocal with a complete absence of instruments except the *shofar*, which never accompanied any vocalization but only served as a signal instrument.[82] In the Temple choral music seems to have dominated, while in the ancient synagogue there appears to have been much more individual or solo performance with responses by the congregation. While Werner may assert that Temple music was nothing but an accessory to its sacrificial ritual,[83] synagogue music was what Curt Sachs called "logogenic" or "word-born."[84] And this word-centered music belonged to nonprofessional, lay leadership—not the professional musicians and clergy who dominated the Temple. As to the style, one must agree with Avenary who reckoned that synagogal styles were "elementary . . . suited to a gathering of people assembled for singing prayer and praise, and for the majority of whom artistically contrived song and complicated tunes were normally out of range. Such congregations had to be cemented together by a kind of music that was easily grasped and performed."[85]

The Influence of Synagogue Music on Christian Practice

Jesus probably attended synagogue services while growing up in Nazareth.[86] Very early in his public ministry he is remembered as having visited the synagogues to pray.[87] It was in the synagogue that he cast out demons,[88] healed the sick,[89] taught,[90] and preached.[91] He is also remembered as having taken a role in synagogal worship—accepting the role of *sheliach tsibbur* for the community and reading from the scroll of Isaiah.[92] The statutory prayers of the synagogue service were so well known to him that he is remembered as having woven them into his teaching.[93] Furthermore, the specific model of prayer that Jesus handed on to his disciples[94] employs prayer idioms common in the synagogue[95] and suggests, again, his familiarity with that setting and its services.

Following the example of Jesus, the disciples continued to frequent the synagogues. There they preached, prayed, and spread the good news.[96] Paul is remembered as having preached his message first in the synagogue.[97] The presence of Jesus' followers in the synagogue was so evident that around 80 C.E. the Jews introduced a malediction against these heretics.[98] This can be considered a significant marker in the relationship between Christians and Jews, and the beginning of the end of their worship together.

While it is true that many followers of Jesus were also present in the Temple until its destruction, Temple cult had little direct influence on emerging Christian worship and song. The synagogue, on the other hand, substantially influenced emerging Christian life, worship, and "music." This non-clerical, lay-led, word-centered worship—with a spiritualized sacrifice of praise at its heart—provided an important model to the followers of Jesus.[99] From a musical perspective, the synagogue was especially influential on the emerging Christian practice of public reading and publicly reciting prayer texts.

CHAPTER THREE NOTES

1. Joseph Gutmann, "Synagogue Origins: Theories and Facts," in *Ancient Synagogues: The State of Research*, Brown Judaic Studies 22, ed. Jacob Neusner et al. (Chico, Calif.: Scholars Press, 1981) 1.

2. Ibid., 2–3.

3. E.g., Philo, *Life of Moses* 3.27.

4. E.g., Josephus, *Jewish War* (ca. 77–78 C.E.) 2.285, 289; 7.44; and *Antiquities of the Jews* (ca. 94 C.E.) 19.300, 305.

5. As a reference to the Jewish building, the word *synagōgē* occurs eight times in Mark, nine times in Matthew, fifteen times in Luke, twice in John, and sixteen times in the Acts of the Apostles. For a complete discussion of these references, see Wolfgang Schrage, "synagōgē," TDNT 7:830–38.

6. See Marilyn Chiat, "First Century Synagogues: Methodological Problems," in Neusner et al., *Ancient Synagogues: The State of Research*, 49–60. In a subsequent volume, Chiat surveys the various archaeological sites that have been identified as ancient synagogues and suggests that only two (Jerusalem: dated to the first century of this era C.E. [p. 202]; and Herodium: stage 1 dated

to the period following Herod's victory in 40 B.C.E. [p. 207]) can be ascribed a first-century existence on the basis of archaeological evidence (Marilyn Joyce Segal Chiat, *Handbook of Synagogue Architecture*, Brown Judaic Studies 29 (Chico, Calif.: Scholars Press, 1982). L. Michael White contends that the synagogue on Delos is probably the oldest; he believes that a private house was renovated for communal use in two stages (the late second century B.C.E. and mid-first century B.C.E.) (L. Michael White, "The Delos Synagogue Revisited," *Harvard Theological Review* 80 [1987] 133–60).

7. Gutmann, "Synagogue Origins," 3–4.

8. See the summary in Marilyn Chiat and Marchita Mauck, "Using Archaeological Sources," in *Two Liturgical Traditions*, vol. 1: *The Making of Jewish and Christian Worship*, ed. Paul Bradshaw and Lawrence Hoffman (Notre Dame, Ind.: University of Notre Dame Press, 1991) 69–80.

9. Andrew Seager, "Ancient Synagogue Architecture: An Overview," in Neusner et al., *Ancient Synagogues: The State of Research*, 41; much of what follows relies upon Seager's summary.

10. Ancient Hebrew did not appear to have a generic term for "music." It seems that in the tenth century C.E. Jewish scholars living in Moorish Spain adapted the Arabic phrase for the "science of music" (*'Ilm al-musiqi*) to form the new Hebrew word *musikah* (Joseph Levine, "Toward Defining the Jewish Prayer Modes with Particular Emphasis on the Adonay Malakh Mode," *Musica Judaica* 3:1 [1980] 21).

11. As Jean-Jacques Nattiez notes, "Examining the borders between music and other symbolic forms along a given continuum reveals that the semantic surface of the concept 'music' is displaced from one culture to another. This is particularly clear in societies [like ancient Israel] for which the word 'music' does not exist" (Jean-Jacques Nattiez, *Music and Discourse: Toward a Semiology of Music*, trans. Carolyn Abbate [Princeton: Princeton University Press, 1990] 54).

12. Many cultures, like ancient Israel, "do not in general have a term for music as a global phenomenon. Instead, they often have words that designate individual musical activities or artifacts, those who sing or play, songs, secular and religious, dance, and other more obscure categories" (Hiromi Lorraine Sakata, *Music in the Mind: The Concepts of Music and Musicians in Afghanistan* [Kent, Ohio: Kent State University Press, 1983] 19). We will employ the word *lyrical* throughout this work as a bridge term that, on the one hand, respects the ambiguity of the nature of what we might want to call "music" in ancient Israel or emerging Christianity, and at the same time finds some resonance in the broad range of our own experiences of "music."

13. For a contemporary example of this distinction, see Gordon Thompson's discussion of the Cāran, some of whom identify their performances as musical, some as non-musical, in "The Cārans of Gujarat: Caste Identity, Music and Cultural Change," *Ethnomusicology* 35 (1991) 388–89.

14. See my "The Cantor in Historical Perspective," *Worship* 56 (1982) 194–213.

15. One witness to democratic prayer leadership in the history of Judaism is reflected in an institution that some believe to be of considerable influence

in the development of the synagogue. The *ma'amadot* (literally "standing men" or bystanders) was a second Temple division of the Israelites into twenty-four groups or watches. Each *ma'amadot*, in weekly rotations, sent representatives to the Temple to "stand by" the priests and Levites during the daily sacrifices. Since only a representative group *(anshe ma'amadot)* was allowed to attend, the rest of the *ma'amadot* "stood by" at home, where, in union with their representatives in Jerusalem, they fasted, prayed, and read those sections of the Torah that related to sacrifice. See S. Zeitlin, "The Origin of the Synagogue," in *Studies in the Early History of Judaism 1* (New York: Ktav, 1973) 77.

16. Idelsohn, *Jewish Music*, 101–2.

17. Joseph Heinemann, *Prayer in the Talmud*, trans. Richard Sarason, Studia Judaica 9 (Berlin and New York: Walter De Gruyter, 1977) 14.

18. "It is true that the priest is the first to read from the Torah, but it would seem that this custom derives from the priest's ancient role as teacher of Torah to the people. There is, however, no halakah which grants him preferential privileges in conducting public worship, such as leading the amidah or the reading of the shema. Nor is being a priest enumerated among the desirable characteristics which a prayer leader should possess (as in *Taanith* 3.2)" (ibid., 117 n. 30).

19. See Lawrence Hoffman, *The Canonization of the Synagogue Service*, Notre Dame Center for the Study of Judaism and Christianity in Antiquity 4 (Notre Dame, Ind., and London: University of Notre Dame Press, 1979) 103–5, and passim.

20. Ismar Elbogen, *Der jüdische Gottesdienst in seiner Entwicklung* (Leipzig: G. Fock, 1913; reprint 1962) 488.

21. Ibid., 483; for a more recent study of this role, see Bernadette Brooten, *Women Leaders in the Ancient Synagogue*, Brown Judaic Studies 36, ed. Jacob Neusner et al. (Chico, Calif.: Scholars Press, 1982), 5–33; also Schrage, "árchisunágōgos," TDNT 7:844–47.

22. Idelsohn, *Jewish Music*, 102; also Brooten who, although not specifically treating the role of the *sheliach tsibbur*, does comment: "Seen in the larger context of women's participation in the life of the ancient synagogue, there is no reason not to take the titles [*archēgos* (leader) elder, mother of synagogue, and priest] as functional, nor to assume that women heads or elders of synagogues had radically different functions than men heads or elders of synagogues. Of the functions outlined for each title, there are none which women could not have carried out" (Brooten, *Women Leaders*, 149). That this perspective was to change radically is illustrated by Rav's harsh statement from the Talmud, "The voice of a woman is indecency" (*B. Berakoth* 24a).

23. The Mishnah, for example, reports: "They arise for prayer. They bring down before the ark an experienced elder, who has children and whose cupboard [house] is empty, so that his heart should be wholly in the prayer. And he says before them 24 blessings: the eighteen said every day, and he adds six more to them" (*Taanith* 2.2). A list of such qualifications was fixed by Rabbi

Judah ben Illai in the second century C.E., which required the emissary to be "a man who has heavy family obligations, who has not enough to meet them, who has to struggle for a livelihood but who nonetheless keeps his house clean, who has an attractive appearance, is humble, pleasant to and liked by people, who has a sweet voice and musical ability, who is well versed in the Scriptures, capable of preaching, conversant with the halakah and haggadah and who knows all the prayers and benedictions by heart" (B. Taanith 16a).

24. See the summary of this evidence in my "The Cantor in Historical Perspective," 198–99.

25. There is some talmudic evidence for certain Levitical singers moving back and forth between Temple and synagogue (e.g., B. Sukkah 53a) which Werner interprets as a movement to "transfer the tradition of the central sanctuary to the country synagogue" (Werner, Sacred Bridge, vol. 1 [New York: Schocken Books 1970 (1959)] 24). Talmudic evidence for first-century C.E. practice greatly weakens the credibility of such an assertion, although one could not rule out completely the possible cross-fertilization between Temple and synagogue. The role of professional Temple singers in the synagogue could not, however, be considered normative in any sense of the word.

26. Heinemann, Prayer in the Talmud, 14. For a radically different view of the place and even existence of statutory prayers in the synagogue at the time of Jesus, see James McKinnon, "On the Question of Psalmody in the Ancient Synagogue," in Early Music History 6, Studies in Medieval and Early Modern Music, ed. Iain Fenlon (Cambridge: Cambridge University Press, 1986), 159–91. See note 42 below for a caution and critique of McKinnon's conclusions.

27. Heinemann, Prayer in the Talmud, 14.

28. Ibid., 64–65.

29. See chapter 2, note 39.

30. As Elbogen notes, "The bare recitation of a profession of faith is too meagre to make up, for any length of time, the only element of a congregational service. It is therefore quite natural that the Biblical sections were enframed in an harmonious introduction and conclusion" (Ismar Elbogen, "Studies in the Jewish Liturgy I," Jewish Quarterly Review 19 [1907] 233).

31. Berakoth 1.4; Megillah 4.3, 5. Josephus notes that the Shema is recited twice each day (Josephus, Antiquities of the Jews 4.18.13). On the antiquity of the Shema as a liturgical unit, see Elbogen, Gottesdienst, 25; this view is challenged by Tzvee Zahavy, who holds for the later emergence of the Shema as a "popular scribal rite," in his "The Politics of Piety," in Bradshaw and Hoffman, The Making of Jewish and Christian Worship, 50–54.

32. On the possible reasons for the exclusion of the Decalogue from the ancient synagogue service, see Reuven Kimelman, "The Sema and Its Blessings: The realization of God's Kingship," in The Synagogue in Late Antiquity, ed. Lee I. Levine (Philadelphia: American Schools of Oriental Research, 1987) 73–86.

33. Heinemann, Prayer in the Talmud, 22; he further suggests that "the custom of reciting precisely eighteen benedictions must have crystallized sometime dur-

ing the century before the destruction of the Temple (at the very latest)'' (224); for a different perspective, see Zahavy who suggests that ''this prayer formed the core of the priestly liturgy sponsored by the patriarchate after the destruction of the Temple'' (Zahavy, ''The Politics of Piety,'' 57).

34. Zahavy is more cautious, suggesting that ''during the initial transition after the destruction of the Temple from about 70 to 90 c.e. the priests promulgated the tefillah and the scribes promoted the shema. . . . In the second phase of development, from about 90 to 155 c.e., the patriarchate sponsored the tefillah to counter a growing scribal faction within the rabbinic movement. . . . In the era from about 155 to 220 c.e. the rabbis amalgamated the shema and the tefillah in a compromise that led to the present shape of the composite rabbinic service'' (Zahavy, ''The Politics of Piety,'' 61–62). For a more traditional view of these elements and their role in the first-century synagogue, see Bouley, *From Freedom to Formula*, 13–28.

35. Heinemann, *Prayer in the Talmud*, 25.

36. I.e., the scroll of the prophet Isaiah was handed to Jesus (Luke 4:17), possibly by the assistant who retrieved the scroll from him in 4:20a; he chose a passage (4:17a); he read the passage; he rolled up the scroll (4:20); he handed the scroll back to the assistant (4:20); he offered a teaching (4:21). One element which Luke does not report was the translation or paraphrase of the reading in Aramaic (targum). This practice was evident before the common era, and arose because of the decline of Hebrew as a spoken language among Jews, especially in the Diaspora but also in Palestine. Written targums appeared by at least the first century c.e. (some, datable from the first century c.e. have been discovered in the caves at Qumran), although ''for some time the rabbis viewed the use of such texts with official disfavor'' (K. G. O'Connell, ''Texts and Versions,'' NJBC 68:103). Since Hebrew was in effect a dead language by 135 c.e. (ibid., 68:101), it is possible to suggest that targums became a standard part of the synagogue liturgy by at least the first third of the second century c.e. Thus the ''Word'' section of the synagogue service included not only a reading, but also its translation and a sermon. See Avigdor Shinan, ''Sermons, Targums and the Reading from Scriptures in the Ancient Synagogue,'' in *The Synagogue in Late Antiquity*, ed. Lee I. Levine (Philadelphia: American Schools of Oriental Research, 1987) 97–110.

37. E.g., Acts 13:27 referring to the former; Acts 15:21 and 2 Corinthians 3:15 referring to the latter.

38. Heinemann, *Prayer in the Talmud*, 228–29.

39. See, for example, *Megillah* 3.4–6; 4.1–2.

40. See Joseph Heinemann, ''The Triennial Lectionary Cycle,'' *Journal of Jewish Studies* 19 (1968) 41–48.

41. See, for example, Anton Arens, *Die Psalmen im Gottesdienst des Alten Bundes: Eine Untersuchung zur Urgeschichte des christlichen Psalmengesanges*, Triere theologische Studien 11 (Trier: Paulinus Verlag, 1961) esp. 160–202.

42. See the useful summary in Massey Shepherd, *The Psalms in Christian Worship* (Collegeville: The Liturgical Press, 1976) 26. James McKinnon summarizes

much of the contemporary scholarship asserting that psalms were not "sung" in the synagogues at the time of Jesus ("On the Question of Psalmody in the Ancient Synagogue"). The caution about McKinnon's work, however, is that in the process of mustering arguments against the singing of psalms in the ancient synagogue, he attempts to demonstrate that the synagogue was devoid of prayer before the destruction of the Temple in 70 C.E. and to suggest that, more important than a liturgical order, what Christian liturgy derives from the synagogue is its "unique liturgical setting of a meeting house for religious associates" (191). McKinnon's conclusions are overdrawn. The synagogue, in my opinion, had a profound effect on emerging Christianity, not only because of its "unique liturgical setting" but because of its unusual style of prayer leadership, its "democratic" model for gathering, and its focus on the Word. McKinnon seems to suggest that there was prayer in ancient Israel everywhere except the synagogue. It is difficult for me to reconcile such a view with ancient Israel's reverence for Torah (which even McKinnon admits was central to synagogue gatherings at the time of Jesus [167]), and the instinct to surround its reading with prayer. Rather than McKinnon's extreme view, I prefer the balance of Heinemann, whom McKinnon cites (nn. 47, 117), but never really addresses.

43. Werner, *Sacred Bridge*, 1:131.

44. Mowinckel, *The Psalms in Israel's Worship*, 1:88.

45. For example, the service "Welcoming the Sabbath," from the traditional Siddur, begins with Psalms 95–99 and 29. See *Prayerbook for Sabbath and Festivals*, trans. and annotated by Philip Birnbaum (New York: Hebrew Publishing Company, 1950) 24–30.

46. Hoffman, *The Canonization of the Synagogue Service*, 127.

47. Heinemann, *Prayer in the Talmud*, ch. 9, "The Fixed Statutory Prayers of the Synagogue," and passim.

48. Philo comments, for example, that the synagogue was a place where the participants performed "hymns, songs and canticles" (Philo, *Against Flaccum* 14). Although he provides no examples of what these might have looked like, see the *psalmi idiotici* composed by the Qumran community collected in Geza Vermes, *The Dead Sea Scrolls in English*, 2d ed. (Middlesex: Penguin Books, 1975) 150–201.

49. Johann Maier, "Zur Verwendung der Psalmen in der synagogalen Liturgie," *Liturgie und Dichtung: Ein interdisziplinäres Kompendium*, ed. H. Becker and R. Kaczynski, 2 vols., Pietas Liturgica 1–2 (Sankt Ottilien: EOS-Verlag, 1983) 1:84.

50. "Take to heart these words which I enjoin on you today. Drill them into your children. Speak of them at home and abroad, whether you are busy or at rest. Bind them at your wrist as a sign and let them be a pendent on your forehead. Write them on the doorposts of your houses and on your gates" (Deut 6:6-9; cf. Ps 1:2).

51. E.g., Leader: "Hear, O Israel"; Congregation: "Hear, O Israel, the Lord our God, the Lord is One." See the summary in Hoffman, *The Canonization of the Synagogue Service*, 47; also, Ismar Elbogen, "Studies in the Jewish Liturgy," *Jewish Quarterly Review* (o.s.) 18 (1906) 587-99.

52. This appears to have been a didactic method for "inducing schoolchildren to memorize biblical verses" (S. Lieberman, ed., *Tosefta Ki-fshutah*, 8 vols. [New York: Jewish Theological Seminary, 1955–73] 3:10–11, as cited in Kimelman, "The Sema and Its Blessings," 81–82).

53. E.g., Leader: "Hear, O Israel, I am the Lord your God"; Congregation: "The Lord our God, the Lord is One." This is the form contained in the midrash Deuteronomy Rabba 2.31 as cited and explained in Kimelman, "The Sema and Its Blessings," 82–83.

54. *Berakoth* 4.4.

55. The period of the *tannaim* can be said to have begun with the destruction of the Temple, ending with the redaction of the Mishnah, i.e., from 70 C.E. to ca. 200. See Neusner, *From Politics to Piety*, especially chs. 6 and 7.

56. Hoffman, *The Canonization of the Synagogue Service*, 50.

57. Elbogen, "Studies II," 709–10.

58. Thus Heinemann comments, "Although there were undoubtedly many people who were not fluent in the fixed prayers . . . and who were thus necessarily dependent on hearing the prayers recited by the Prayer Leader in order to fulfill their obligation, nevertheless, their participation through listening was of an active nature, which found expression in the frequent responses: 'Amen,' 'Blessed be the Lord to whom blessing is due forever and ever,' 'May his great name be eternally blessed,' 'Blessed be the name of his glorious kingdom for all eternity,' etc." (Heinemann, *Prayer in the Talmud*, 16).

Philo's description of the Therapeutae (*On the Contemplative Life* 10) offers evidence that responsorial forms were common at least in some sectors of Judaism at the time. "Then the president rises and sings a hymn composed as an address to God, either a new one of his own composition or an old one by prophets of an earlier day . . . while all the rest listen in complete silence except when they have to chant the closing lines or refrains, for then they all lift up their voices, men and women alike" (in *Philo*, 10 vols., The Loeb Classical Library, trans. F. H. Colson [Cambridge: Harvard University Press, 1941] 9:163).

59. Hanoch Avenary, "Music," EJ 12:578.

60. These are sometimes referred to as *nusaḥim*. The term is problematic, however, since it seems to connote a given text and not necessarily the intonation of that text. See the discussion in Levine, *The Synagogue in Late Antiquity*, 14–15.

61. Idelsohn, *Jewish Music*, 73; although Idelsohn put forth this theory in the 1920s, "to date, no convincing argument has been advanced to refute Idelsohn's demonstrated correlation between the prayer modes and Scriptural cantillation" (Levine, *The Synagogue in Late Antiquity*, 19).

62. Avenary, "Music," EJ 12:578; for some examples of contemporary prayer modes thought to reflect traditional Jewish music, see ibid., 12:581.

63. *B. Sanhedrin* 99a.

64. Avenary, "Music," EJ 12:577, in reference to *B. Megillah* 3a.

65. *B. Megillah* 32a.

66. Werner, "Jewish Music," NGDMM 9:623.

67. See Solange Corbin, *L'église à la conquête de sa musique,* Pour la Musique, ed. Roland-Manuel (Paris: Gallimard, 1960) 42.

68. Avenary, "Jewish Music," 1:995. Werner distinguishes a threefold variety in the way of publicly rendering readings: plain recitation (spoken), ecphonesis (*Sprechgesang,* or a semi-musical recitative), and cantillation (regular musical chant). He goes on to suggest that it is virtually impossible to distinguish between the last two forms. He concludes that "the 'primitive,' acoustically unorganized rendering of Scripture is not easily accessible to musical evaluation and classification" (Werner, *Sacred Bridge,* 1:104). This conclusion is collaborated by Edith Gerson-Kiwi, who believes that cantillation is first of all amplification of the word employing a restricted number of sounds, governed by the verbal rhythm in phrases devoid of any metrical structure. Cantillation, therefore, is not a melodic ornament, and still less a genuine musical composition, since the text is pronounced rapidly to the degree of flexibility permitted by the nature of the language involved (Edith Gerson-Kiwi, "Musique (dans la Bible): La lecture biblique (cantillation)," *Dictionnaire de la Bible: Supplément* [Paris: Letouzey et Ané, 1957], 5:1449–64, as summarized in Giulio Cattin, *Music of the Middle Ages 1,* trans. Steven Botterill [Cambridge: Cambridge University Press, 1984] 8).

69. For a discussion of some of these various modes as they occurred in more recent usage, see Idelsohn, *Jewish Music,* 35–91.

70. The increased importance of the reading of the Torah seems to be demonstrated by architectural changes in the synagogue (Seager, "Ancient Synagogue Architecture," 43).

71. Avenary, "Music," EJ 12:583.

72. These accents seem to have replaced a series of conventional hand and finger gestures called *chironomy* that (until the introduction of written accents) had been the traditional way to signal the places for musical cadences in the texts. See Avenary, "Jewish Music," 1:995.

73. From the Greek *ekphōneō,* to "call out" or "declaim"; the term was coined by Isaac Tzetzes, *Parnassos* 9 (1885) 441, as cited in Gudrun Engberg, NGDMM 6:99.

74. Avenary, "Music," EJ 12:583. This phenomenon occurred at about the same time that Jewish scholars (Masoretes) began adding vowel symbols to the consonantal spelling that, until that time, had been used for writing Hebrew and other Semitic languages. The result of this process was the emergence of the Masoretic text of the Old Testament. See, for example, the introduction by H. M. Orlinsky, "The Masoretic Text: Fact or Fiction," in the facsimile reprint of Christian David Ginsburg, *Introduction to the Massoretico-Critical Edition of the Hebrew Bible* (New York: Ktav, 1966).

75. See Avenary, "Music," EJ 12:584.

76. Werner, "Jewish Music," NGDMM 9:624.

77. Suzanne Haïk-Vantoura, *The Music of the Bible Revealed,* trans. Dennis Weber, ed. John Wheeler (Berkeley: Bibal Press, 1991).

78. See, for example, Hanoch Avenary, *The Ashkenazi Tradition of Biblical Chant between 1500 and 1900* (Tel-Aviv: Tel-Aviv University, 1978).

79. Werner, "Jewish Music," NGDMM 9:624. The best single collection of transcriptions of various forms of cantillation continues to be that of A. Z. Idelsohn, *Hebräisch-orientalische Melodienschatz zum erste Male Gesammelt*, 10 vols. (Leipzig: Breitkopf & Härtel, 1914–32).

80. Of the numerous references to the *shofar* in the Mishnah, only a few make specific reference to its use in the synagogue, e.g., *Rosh ha-Shanah* 3.7; 4.5–9; and *Taanith* 2.3–4.

81. Werner, "Jewish Music," NGDMM 9:623.

82. Werner, "Musical Instruments," IDB 3:473.

83. Werner, "Music," IDB 3:459.

84. Curt Sachs, *The Rise of Music in the Ancient World* (New York: W. W. Norton and Company, 1943) 52.

85. Avenary, "Music," EJ 12:571.

86. Luke 4:16 notes that Jesus attended the synagogue in Nazareth "according to his custom"; on the interpretation of this phrase in view of Jesus' upbringing, see Gustaf Hermann Dalman, *Jesus-Jeshua: Studies in the Gospels* (New York: McMillan, 1929) 33–34, 40.

87. Luke 4:16.

88. Mark 1:23-27 (Luke 4:33-36); Mark 1:39.

89. Matt 4:23; Mark 3:1-5 (Matt 12:9-13; Luke 6:6-10); Matt 9:35; Luke 13:10-17.

90. Matt 4:23; Matt 9:35; Luke 13:10.

91. Mark 1:39; Matt 9:35.

92. Luke 4:16.

93. E.g., the section from the Shema in Matthew 22:37.

94. Luke 11:2-4 = Matt 6:9-13.

95. Heinemann, *Prayer in the Talmud*, 63; on the "anti-synagogal" nature of the Lord's Prayer, however, see Joseph Heinemann, "The Background of Jesus' Prayer in the Jewish Liturgical Tradition," in *The Lord's Prayer and Jewish Liturgy*, ed. Jakob Petuchowski and Michael Brocke (New York: Crossroad Book, 1978) 81–89.

96. Acts 9:20; 13:5, 15; 14:1; 17:1, 10, 17; 18:4, 19, 26; 19:8.

97. Acts 9:19-20.

98. On the *birkat-ha-minim* see W. Horbury, "The Benediction of the Minim and Early Jewish Christian Controversy," *Journal of Theological Studies* 33 (1982) 19–61; as to whether or not this "malediction" was directed specifically or exclusively at Christians, see Reuven Kimelman, "Birkat Haminim and the Lack of Evidence for an Anti-Christian Prayer in Late Antiquity," in *Jewish and Christian Self-Definition*, vol. 2, *Aspects of Judaism in the Graeco-Roman Period*, ed. E. P. Sanders, A. I. Baumgarten, and Alan Mendelson (London: SCM Press, 1980) 226–44, 392–403.

99. See, for example, my discussion of the Christian adaptation of the *sheliach tsibbur* in "The Cantor in Historical Perspective," 202–4.

4 Borrowed Spaces and Emerging Christianity
(First Century C.E.)

The "Setting"

Unlike many peoples of the surrounding region, ancient Israel did not restrict its worship to a single location or type of building. It is true that, until its destruction in 70 C.E., the Temple was the center of Jewish sacrifice, and synagogues became important centers for prayer and study by the second century B.C.E. Prayer was not confined, however, to these two institutions. A pious Jew was expected to pray in every place and at every time.[1] This meant that breaking bread, seeing lightning, purchasing a vessel, or watching the sun set were all occasions for blessing God.[2] Virtually every and any location was an appropriate setting for offering a blessing; yet the home—like the Temple and synagogues—was a privileged place for prayer. This was especially true since the home was the central setting for meals which were always sacred events for Jews.

Jesus' table ministry can be considered one of the most characteristic acts of his ministry,[3] as well as the context in which the disciples experienced him as the Risen One.[4] Thus, it is appropriate to suggest that Christianity was born around the table. It is significant, however, that Christianity did not emerge around any single table, or in any particular kind of house or dwelling. There is, historically speaking, no aboriginal "mother church" in Christianity. Rather, Christianity arose around many tables, in a variety of private and public settings.[5] Such is the model provided by Jesus himself, who moved from place to place and table to table. The diversity of the settings for his ministry is remarkable: homes of the rich, borrowed rooms, public inns, houses of tax collectors, and even grassy hillsides.[6] What is most notable is that none of them belonged to him.

Like Jesus, his first followers did not confine their prayer or table ministry to any single place or type of dwelling. The palatial homes of wealthy believers,[7] the more modest dwellings of poorer disciples,[8] ancient apartments,[9] public rooms[10] and hillsides provided them with the temporary settings they required for their gatherings. There the word was proclaimed, teaching imparted, and healing offered. It was in such places that the members of this first community gathered especially for the breaking of the bread.

It seems that none of these places were permanent worship sites or used exclusively for cultic purposes. Rather, the followers of Jesus seemed to have moved and adapted their worship spaces according to need.[11] It is clear that whatever structure offered shelter to the early community was not considered the "house of God." Rather, the Christian community itself was the first and only *oikos tou Theou*.[12] The only true Christian architecture of the first century was one of living stones and not of brick or mortar. This community-centered ideal accompanied the development of Christianity from its rural Jewish origins into the urban Gentile mission.

The First Christian "Musicians"

Any attempt to speak about "musicians" in emerging Christianity is an exercise in anachronism. This is true, first of all, because of the previously noted auditory environment of New Testament Christianity which challenges and stretches our definition of "music" and, by extension, "musician." It is also true because of the New Testament's silence not only about any "musical" office, but also about virtually every cultic office. Although we know, for example, that the community gave thanks over bread and wine from the earliest times[13] we are never told who presided, or whether such presidency was continuously invested in one individual. Raymond Brown summarizes:

> The only thing of which we can be reasonably sure is that someone must have presided at the eucharistic meals, and that those who participated acknowledged his right to preside. How one got the right to preside and whether it endured beyond a single instance we do not know; but a more plausible substitute for the chain theory is the thesis that sacramental "powers" were part of the mission of the church and that there were diverse ways in which the church designated individuals to exercise those powers—the essential element always being church or community consent (which was tantamount to ordination).[14]

FIGURE 3. HOUSE OF POMPEII
Plan of the house of Pansa, Pompeii, second century B.C.E., after Helen
Gardner, *Art through the Ages*, 8th rev. ed. by Horst de la Croix and Richard
Tansey (Hartcourt, Brace, Jovanovich, San Diego, 1986) p. 174.

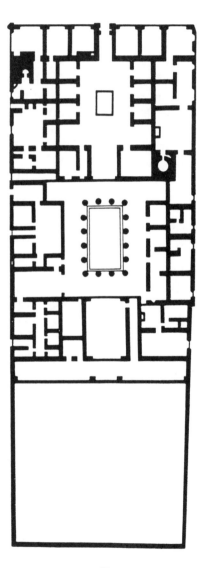

This phenomenon of a prayer-action led by an unspecified minister is the rule for the primitive Christian community. We know that some spoke in tongues (1 Cor 14:2), some prophesied (1 Cor 14:3), some interpreted (1 Cor 14:5), some responded "amen" to another's thanksgiving (1 Cor 14:16), and some sang (Eph 5:19) or read (Col 4:16). No office is ever connected with these prayer-actions. We know that there were prayers, songs, and readings, but we do not know who led them. This consistent lack of evidence, coupled with the previously discussed wide-ranging acquaintance of the primitive community with the *sheliach tsibbur* in synagogue worship, plus the very acceptance of such leadership by Jesus and Paul in the synagogue, suggests that volunteer prayer leadership continued in the emerging Christian cult.

Werner contends that "Jewish chant must have been transmitted to the Christian church mainly by cantors, to whom there are some epitaphs in the Roman catacombs."[15] This hypothesis, though interesting, is nonetheless problematic for the New Testament period for a number of reasons. First and foremost, as previously demonstrated, there was no "cantor," properly speaking, in the synagogues of the first century C.E. Second, Werner's failure to identify the specific epitaphic evidence to support this contention makes it difficult to substantiate. Third, the epitaphic evidence that can be identified cannot be dated from the first century C.E. Thus, while it is appropriate to acknowledge the influence of synagogue "music" on that of emerging Christianity, it seems inappropriate to identify any permanent musician or "cantor" as the ordinary transmitter of such influence.

Emerging Christian Song

Establishing the kinds of texts that were "sung" in the emerging Christian community is more complex than endeavoring to do the same for the synagogue or Temple of the first century C.E. One practical reason for this is the existence of the New Testament, which provides us with an abundance of textual evidence for the new religion. A second reason is the unconventional nature of emerging Christianity which, while maintaining clear continuity with Judaism, was also in radical discontinuity with that tradition. Third, the extemporaneous nature of Jesus' own speech—which Amos Wilder characterized as dynamic, actual, immediate, and reckless of posterity[16]—as well as the corresponding revolution in the language of his disciples contributed to the evolution of new forms and a heightened proclivity for improvisation in the New Testament period.

We will consider various types of texts under the headings of: short praise formulae, fragments and acclamations, infancy canticles, God-hymns,[17] Christological hymns,[18] psalms, readings, and table prayers.

Short Praise Formulae

Very often in early Christian writings one encounters short, standardized phrases praising God.[19] These *kurze Lobsprüche*, which appear to have developed from Jewish prayer forms, are generally called *berakoth* in Judaism.[20] In Christian writings three types of short praise formulae are distinguishable by their respective *Grundwort*: doxology (*doxa*), eulogy (*eulogia*), and the thanks-formula (*charis*).

While there is common agreement that doxologies exist in the New Testament, there is little unanimity when it comes to defining the nature of a doxology. Some hold that some form of the word *doxa* or its equivalent is a defining element of all doxologies[21] while others do not.[22] Following Reinhard Deichgräber, who designates *doxology* as any short *Lobsprüche* that agrees with the base form ''to (him) be glory for ever,''[23] it is possible to identify twenty doxologies in the New Testament.[24]

The eulogy can be considered a *berakah* in the narrow sense of the word.[25] Like the doxology, this form originated in Judaism and then was taken over and transformed by Christianity. The New Testament gives us seven *berakoth*.[26]

The thanks-formulae are those short phrases of thanksgiving found in the Pauline literature that contain a proclamation of thanks, generally succeeded by the reasons for the thanks.[27] Such language, like that of the other short praise formulae, is characteristically emphatic and proclamatory. More so than the doxology or eulogy forms, the thanks-formula appears to be a mixture of Greek and Jewish elements, and uniquely Christian. There are at least six New Testament passages that can be considered thanks-formulae.[28]

Fragments and Acclamations

The New Testament also contains what Ralph Martin calls ''Jewish-Christian fragments and ejaculations.''[29] These popular acclamations were naive expressions of belief, "... untainted by theological arguments; the primitive Christian community had not yet established an organized worship. Its spontaneous acclamations represented the active part that the congregation played during the first two centuries, when no more than the core of the liturgy was in existence."[30] Klaus-Peter Jörns believes that such fragments are a key to understanding the interactive and "responsorial" nature of early Christian worship.[31] There are at least five such fragments and/or acclamations in the New Testament. The most common is "amen," which concludes prayers and doxologies,[32] prophecy, letters, and writings.[33] The acclamation "halleluia" appears to function as a doxology in the New Testament.[34] A third fragment is "hosanna," which arises in the accounts of Jesus' triumphal entry into Jerusalem[35] where it appears to be a spontaneous acclamation.[36] "Marana tha," which occurs only in 1 Corinthians 16:22, is another fragment. Finally, the term "abba"—an Aramaic emphatic form of 'ab (father) that was used by Jesus 170 times in the Gospels[37]—seems to have been taken over very early into worship, possibly as a "spirit-inspired cry,"[38] as demonstrated by its usage in certain epistles.[39]

Infancy Canticles

In his study *The Birth of the Messiah*, Raymond Brown identifies four Lukan passages as infancy canticles.[40] The first of these is the Magnificat (Luke 1:46-55), a "catena of Old Testament reminiscences,"[41] not of Lukan origin, which was probably composed in a Jewish-Christian context.[42] Brown and others further intimate that this hymn was used liturgically in the early community.[43] A second is the Benedictus (Luke 1:67-79). Like the Magnificat, the Benedictus was probably a Jewish-Christian rather than a Lukan composition. The Gloria in excelsis (Luke 2:14), though numbered by some among the New Testament doxologies, also needs to be considered in the context of the other infancy canticles. Like the others, this canticle was probably a pre-Lukan composition that might have sprung from a community of Jewish-Christian *anawim*.[44] Drawing on a parallel in the Qumran community, Brown comments that "if the Qumran Anawim could compose hymns for the angels to sing, so could a Christian community of similar piety and liturgical interests."[45] He even concedes that the Gloria and the parallel in Luke 19:38 "could constitute antiphonal responses."[46] Finally, the Nunc dimittis (Luke 2:29-32) is another hymn that seems to have been composed by

Jewish-Christian *anawim*.[47] Its lyric character, like that of the other infancy canticles, suggest its cultic employment at an early stage in the development of Christian worship.

God-Hymns

A second category of larger hymnic forms in the New Testament is that of the God-hymns. These are distinguished from the short praise formulae by their length and from the Christological hymns by their lack of any reference to Christ. Although there are only a few God-hymns that survive in the New Testament,[48] Deichgräber contends that this type of hymn played a significant role in emerging Christianity.[49] He bases this contention on the fact that many times the New Testament mentions that God is to be praised,[50] that there are many short praise formulae in the New Testament that could be remnants of larger pieces, and that Judaism—with its large number of hymns and hymn fragments—provided both the models and the impetus for the development of these larger hymnic forms.[51]

Christological Hymns

A final category of larger hymn types is the Christological hymn. In offering his definition of a Christological hymn, Deichgräber emphasizes two elements: (1) the content of such a hymn is Christ and his work, and (2) the language, style, and structure are clearly poetic.[52] Yet here as with other lyric elements in the New Testament, there is no unanimity among scholars when it comes to designating Christological hymns or hymnic sections.[53]

This discrepancy is magnified a hundredfold when one moves from the difficult task of identification to the perilous position of predicating a cultic usage of such elements. Thus the caution of Gerhard Delling is well remembered:

> Attempts have been made to identify various primitive Christian hymns or hymnal fragments in the New Testament. But such identifications must remain hypothetical, particularly as there is in the New Testament no attempt—and this is a pivotal point worth noting in itself—to use the Greek style of metrical hymns. The pieces in the New Testament which take the form of praise are in general so little controlled by any clearly discernible laws that for the most part judgment as to their character as hymns can claim only limited validity.[54]

Such healthy skepticism is apparent in the many biblical scholars who are unwilling to accept the attestations of their colleagues concerning hymnic materials in the New Testament. Many are the commentators who disagree that hymnic elements exist, or who ignore the question altogether. Yet even Delling for all his caution admits to "many hymn-like passages in primitive Christian liturgy," recognizes that "it is possible that improvised songs were sung in the service," and affirms that some New Testament passages (e.g., 1 Tim 3:16) are plainly "old hymns."[55]

It is not possible to affirm that all of the short praise formulae, fragments and acclamations, infancy canticles, God-hymns, and Christological hymns outlined above were employed in ancient Christian worship or would have been recognizable as "musical" elements when they were. Yet, given what we know about the auditory environment of first-century C.E. Palestine, the many lyric elements of Jewish worship, the influence of Jewish worship on the followers of Jesus, the explosion of newly composed psalms and hymns in various segments of first-century C.E. Judaism such as the community at Qumran,[56] the ecstatic nature of the Christian kerygma, as well as the multiple New Testament passages that have been identified at one time or another as lyric, hymnic, or song-like,[57] it is very probable that these or similar texts did punctuate the emerging Christian cult and could be considered "musical" elements of that cult in the broad sense of that term. This leads us to agree with Joseph Gelineau that there must have been "an intense lyrical quality in the life of the Apostolic church."[58]

Psalms

We have already illustrated the tenuous role that psalmody played in synagogue worship at the dawn of Christianity. In our previous discussion we concluded that, while the spirit of prayer embodied in the psalms may have influenced synagogal prayer in the first century C.E., it is questionable whether psalms were commonly sung in first-century synagogue worship.

While there is more basis for giving some role to sung psalmody in emerging Christian worship, its place in that cult is yet quite ambiguous. Such ambiguity stems from the fact that the psalms are, on the one hand, the Old Testament book most frequently cited in the New Testament.[59] Yet, on the other hand, their presence in

Christian worship is not explicitly noted before the end of the second century C.E.[60]

As in the synagogues of the era, it is possible that the psalms served as a book of readings for the early Christian community.[61] It is also possible that the psalms—some of which were traditional for home rituals like the Passover[62]—found a place in the new home rituals of the followers of Jesus. The "Passover memory" that shaped emerging Christian table practice[63] could have contributed to this development. What was probably more determinative for the adoption of psalmody in this early period, however, was the previously noted revolutionary style of Jesus' preaching, which evoked a similar revolution in the language of his disciples. If the preaching of the early community had more in common with town criers or auctioneers than traditionally understood rabbinic discourse and if, as Dodd contends, Jesus was revealed through oral tradition and charismatic experience,[64] then it would not be surprising that, in this heightened auditory environment, the new followers of the Way sought poetic expression for their faith. Fragments from the psalms might have found their way into preaching or proclamation, new psalm-like compositions emerged, and traditional biblical psalms were reinterpreted in light of the Jesus experience. Given the wide diversity of first-century C.E. practice, however, it would be hazardous to suggest that there was any set pattern for employing psalms within Christian worship.

Readings

There are numerous New Testament indicators that reading quickly developed as a statutory element in early Christian worship. For example, the well-known precedent from the Jewish synagogues of the day found no rejection in the New Testament, which remembered Jesus taking a central role in the proclamation of the word.[65] Certain passages, like the story of the two disciples on the road to Emmaus,[66] suggest a word and table sequence that is an unquestionable pattern of Christian worship by the second century.[67] Furthermore, the New Testament explicitly mentions public reading a number of times.[68] Such references are related to New Testament evidence that the "Word of God" is understood not only as the Old Testament,[69] but also as the word of Jesus,[70] as Jesus himself,[71] and even the word about Jesus.[72] This expanded understanding of the Word of God suggests what might have been "read"[73] in the gatherings of the primitive community, namely, sections from the Old Testament, sayings or stories of or about Jesus as they took written form, and various pastoral letters, like those of Paul. Maybe most telling for the emergence of this statutory element is the rise of the written gospel itself.

Table Prayers

A final genre of texts that served the rising lyricism of the Christian community was the table prayer that accompanied their emerging Eucharistic practice. For a pious Jew, no meal experience could begin without the breaking of bread and an accompanying *berakah*.[74] On Sabbaths and festivals this pre-meal blessing found a post-meal complement in the extended blessing known as the *birkat hamazzon*.[75] These traditions were well known to the Jewish followers of Jesus who borrowed and adapted them.[76] Although the meal proper eventually separated from this ritual in the Christian community,[77] the prayers remained and contributed to the evolution of what we know as Eucharistic Prayers.

"Song" Forms

In our discussion of Jewish precedents, we noted that there is more surety about ancient Jewish prayer forms than there is about their melodic or rhythmic structure. A similar remark could be made about ancient Christian "song." Consequently, we will concentrate more on the forms of the "music," and offer an occasional reflection about melodic or rhythmic elements.

Short Praise Formulae

These brief forms often have the character of a conclusion. It is possible that, for example, the doxology originally served as a response to a preaching event and as such passed into the Christian assemblies and organized worship.[78] There is a strong link between the doxology and the "amen": of the twenty doxologies we identified in the New Testament, only three do not conclude with an "amen."[79] Two of the eulogies we identified also function as a concluding pattern and are wed to the "amen."[80] Although none of the "thanks-formulae" we identified are followed by "amen" in the text, some do function as concluding formularies,[81] and could have been sealed by "amen." This hypothesis is supported not only by the emphatic and spontaneous nature of these formulae, but also by the notable reference in 1 Corinthians 14:16 in which Paul urges the community to prayer in such a way so that others can comprehend and "say 'amen' to your thanksgiving." Delling summarizes the liturgical usage of the doxology—a summary applicable to all of these formulae: "The usage was . . . not invented, presumably, in the letter writing of the primitive church, but was imported from elsewhere. And the most obvious place of origin is in worship: for rounding off teaching, exhortation and prepared discourses, an expression of praise was most suitable. It gave the congregation the opportunity to make the message its own, to acknowledge it as binding by its amen."[82]

As to the musical quality of these short formulae, they are better understood as joyous outbursts and spontaneous acclamations than sustained musical events. These are more liturgical "shouts" than "songs."

Fragments and Acclamations

Even more than the short praise formulae did the fragments and acclamations enumerated above serve as spontaneous shouts in the emerging worship of the early Christian community. Their brevity and emphatic quality suggest a heightened unpredictability about their usage. It is true that, as previously noted, the "amen" often served to conclude the prayer or preaching of another and—at least in the synagogues of the time—was an essential sign of the congregation's involvement in the worship.[83] The "amen" was, undoubtedly, a key response in emerging Christian worship as well.[84] There is also evidence that the "halleluia" served as a concluding response, in both Judaism[85] and early Christianity.[86] It is also possible that "hosanna," which apparently served as a congregational response in the primitive community,[87] sometimes served as a concluding acclamation. Yet more than predictable cultic rejoinders to well-known cues, these are textual remnants of the spontaneous cries that punctuated the rites of the nascent Christian community.

Infancy Canticles, God-Hymns and Christological Hymns

It is not possible to demonstrate, beyond a reasonable doubt, that all of these larger "hymn" forms—or even that any of them—found

77

an enduring place in emerging Christian worship.[88] What seems clear, however, is that such larger hymnic forms—similar to those that do survive in the various strata of the New Testament—were characteristic of the evolving cult. The very survival of so many larger hymnic remnants in the New Testament seems incontestable evidence for this assertion.

As to how such hymns were performed, or what they sounded like, one can only guess. The presumed presence of volunteer prayer leaders—Christian counterparts to the *sheliach tsibbur*—suggests that some of these larger forms may have been improvised by a leader, with the assembly repeating each line in turn.[89] It is even more probable that—given the length of some of these texts as well as the fluid state of their content in the oral mode—such hymns were performed by a volunteer prayer leader while the assembly added some phrases of blessing or affirmation, at least at the end of the prayer.[90] It is also conceivable that some of these hymns were performed as solos, without congregational response. The caution with this last suggestion, however, is eloquently offered by Paul himself, who counsels the Corinthian community to seek only those gifts that build up the community. He continues, "I will pray with the spirit and I will pray with the mind also; I will sing with the spirit and I will sing with the mind also. Otherwise, if you bless with the spirit, how can any one in the position of an outsider say the 'amen' to your thanksgiving when he does not know what you are saying" (1 Cor 14:15-16; RSV). Paul's admonition suggests that while there were, undoubtedly, situations in which individuals gave singular voice to hymns in communal worship, it is improbable that such singular hymnody was emblematic of the evolving cult. Even more unlikely is the possibility that any soloist would have been able to suppress the community's affirmation of such spirited praise.[91]

Establishing the melodic or rhythmic contour of these larger forms is virtually impossible. However, Avenary's suggestion of "prayer modes"—plastic enough to fit such fluid prose texts[92]—offers one possible model for conceiving how such hymns may have been performed.[93]

Psalms

The previously noted ambiguity concerning the place of psalms in emerging Christian worship makes suggesting anything about their performance a relatively precarious enterprise. If the psalms continued to function as a book of readings for the early Christian community, then their performance style would be similar to that of other cultic readings.[94] If the psalms found a place in the new home rituals of the followers of Jesus it is probable that their form dictated the style of their performance: some could have been led by an individual with others joining on a refrain after each colon; others could have employed a responsorial form in which the congregation responded to each verse with some brief refrain; the assembly might have punctuated other psalms with cries of "halleluia"; it is even possible that some texts were rendered strophically.[95] As to the musical nature of such forms, no one is sure.[96] Idelsohn and his disciples would like to suggest that musical forms yet extant in the nineteenth and early twentieth centuries are suggestive of sounds from the dawn of Christianity.[97] It is an interesting, even credible, but nonetheless unprovable hypothesis.

Readings

As we have already noted, readings from various sections of the Hebrew Scriptures were rendered by different musical modes or formulae in the ancient synagogue.[98] Whatever modes were in existence at the rise of Christianity were probably borrowed by the followers of Jesus—especially the Jewish Christians—for the cultic proclamation of the Hebrew Scriptures. When Gentile communities began the cultic proclamation of readings from the Hebrew Scriptures it is probable that they borrowed at least the idea if not the melodic and rhythmic structure of the Hebrew modes for cantillation. This suggestion finds support in the fact that there appear to be no other models outside of Judaism in the ancient world for such cantillation.[99] As to the "musical" settings for the other elements that were "read," one may suggest that (borrowing Werner's categories)[100] such public proclamations migrated from ecphonesis (or a semi-musical recitative) to cantillation (regular musical chant) as they were more clearly identified as the "word of the Lord." Given that Christianity gave birth to new genres of God's word—the Gospels and Epistles—so too did these genres eventually develop distinctive musical formulae that were related to but different from their Jewish predecessors.[101] Such was especially true as the Gentile community came to prominence in the new religion.[102]

Table Prayers

Just as Jews could not simply speak a public reading or declaim a public prayer without some level of musicality, so it was not possible for them to enact the rituals surrounding their meals without "music." The context of these meal prayers[103] as well as their structure suggest that they were led by a single individual, with responses from the assembled family.[104] The followers of Jesus adopted and adapted this practice, retaining much of its structure and content, but interpreting it in view of the Jesus experience,[105] something that Jesus himself probably did at the Last Supper. Even when the meal proper was separated from the prayer the same performance practice seems to have endured. In attempting to discover what such prayers might have sounded like, we again have recourse to the previously discussed "prayer modes," which would have been flexible enough to fit such fluid prose texts.[106]

Instruments

We have already noted how instrumental music (apart from the *shofar*) never found a place in synagogue worship. Thus the precedent for what in another age would be called "a cappella" worship did not originate with the followers of Jesus, but with the rabbis who effectively prohibited the use of all instrumental music in Jewish worship until the nineteenth century. It was this spirit that permeated emerging Christian worship from its inception.

While there are many references to instruments in the New Testament,[107] such references—aside from some in Revelation—never mention them in terms of the emerging Christian cult. Even though Johannes Quasten[108] and other, earlier writers accept the references in Revelation as proof that instruments were employed in the first-century cult, contemporary scriptural scholarship calls for a more symbolic interpretation of these passages.

The reasons for the absence of instrumental music (probably even the *shofar*) from Christian worship are complex. Almost all would agree that one contributing element is a consistent affirmation of the primacy of vocal music in emerging Christianity. It is the word-event, the parable, the kerygma that is central—to such an extent that even the meal could be spiritualized without anything essential being lost. In such a context, instrumental music would not play a critical role. Some have also suggested that there was a conscious rejection of this music. Thus Werner, commenting on 1 Corinthians 13, writes: "Explicitly stated here is the primacy of vocal performance over any instrumental music. Implicit is the contempt of all instrumental music, and the emphatic disparagement of 'gong' and cymbals, two of the Temple's percussion instruments. . . . In general [Paul] considers all musical instruments lifeless or soulless (1 Cor 14:7)."[109]

James McKinnon would appear to disagree, suggesting that "a doctrine of opposition to instruments" in the Christian community did not develop until the third and fourth centuries. On the contrary, Christian music was so exclusively vocal in its early stages that the occasion to criticize the use of instruments in church never arose.[110] McKinnon, however, probably overstates his case. While it is true that, as McKinnon notes, early Christianity was in continuity with the synagogue service, he fails to acknowledge that the synagogue and the Temple were complementary elements in first-century Judaism. Emerging Christianity had a much more tenuous relationship to the Temple which, although never completely rejected, was a place of increasing tension for the disciples. Furthermore, Temple sacrifice, which was essential to Jewish cult, became increasingly peripheral for emerging Christianity, especially with the mission to the Gentiles. Thus, I would suggest that there was an element of "rejection" in Christianity's earliest assessment of instrumental music: a rejection wed to a growing rejection of the type of priesthood, cult, and religious view embodied in the Temple.

Werner establishes a correlation between sacrifice, hierarchy, and art music, on the one hand, and logos worship, rudimentary democracy, and folk-song on the other.[111] Instrumental music more clearly allies with the former, and a cappella music with the latter. The absence of instrumental music in the primitive Christian community, therefore, is not simply due to its having no other option. Rather, it seems intimately wed to the embrace of democratic forms of worship, a rejection of Temple priesthood and sacrifice, and to the process of spiritualization[112] that marked the emerging cult.

Summary on "Christian Music" of the First Century C.E.

In discussing the evolving cult of the early Christian community, Thomas Talley once remarked that early Christian practice reflects patterns which are as meticulously different from, as they are broadly grounded on, Jewish tradition. Talley's observation is useful when

81

attempting to summarize Christian music of the first century C.E. There is, for example, much continuity in terms of texts, musical forms, styles of "musical" leadership, and melodic building blocks, especially between Jewish synagogue, home rituals, and emerging Christian cult. Many of the texts that were part of the lyrical horizon of early Christian worship (like the infancy canticles) were borrowed from Judaism; the practice of publicly cantillating readings is distinctively Jewish, and even the priority of vocal music to the exclusion of instruments was a synagogal innovation. Yet the tonal landscape of early Christianity cannot be understood simply in terms of continuity with Jewish synagogal or domestic worship. Texts were borrowed and adapted, the nature of public reading was redefined in terms of Gospel and Epistle, and the traditional patterns of Jewish chants—already under the influence of Hellenism—were increasingly influenced by the musical traditions of Gentile believers.[113]

Maybe more significant than any of these for emerging Christian song was the previously stressed ecstatic nature of this new kerygma and cult. Taking its cue from the speech of Jesus which appears to have been radically different from that of other Jewish teachers of the time, we noted the extemporaneous, improvisatory, and dynamic nature of the early Christian kerygma. Thus spontaneity and immediacy of expression were hallmarks of the early kerygma and, by extension, early worship. Therefore, while maintaining a certain continuity with synagogal and domestic Jewish precedents, Christian cult was nonetheless revolutionary and distinctively charismatic. This suggests an intense lyricism in early Christian worship, which prized responsorial forms,[114] punctuated as it was by shouts, acclamations, hymns, improvised chants, and even the gift of tongues.[115]

NOTES FOR CHAPTER FOUR

1. "A man is obliged to recite one hundred benedictions each day" (*B. Menahot* 43b).

2. See, for example, the discussion of these short formularies in Louis Bouyer, *Eucharist: Theology and Spirituality of the Eucharistic Prayer*, trans. Charles Quinn (Notre Dame, Ind., and London: University of Notre Dame Press, 1968), 55–58.

3. See, for example, Schillebeeckx, *Jesus*, 217.

4. See, for example, the summary by Raymond Brown in "The Resurrection in John 21—Missionary and Pastoral Directives for the Church," *Worship* 64 (1990) 438–39.

5. Acts of the Apostles, for example, speaks of the movement "from house to house" (8:3; 20:20).

6. For an overview of the table imagery and Jesus' table ministry in the New Testament, see Geoffrey Wainwright, *Eucharist and Eschatology* (London: Epworth Press, 1971) 25–42; a more focused introduction to food and meal in the Gospel of Luke is provided by Robert J. Karris in *Luke: Artist and Theologian* (New York: Paulist Press, 1985) 47–78.

7. For example, the excavated villa at Anaploga, dated to the time of Paul, which Jerome Murphy-O'Connor believes is "the sort of house in which Gaius acted as host to Paul and the whole church (Romans 16:23)" (Jerome Murphy-O'Connor, "The Corinth that Saint Paul Saw," *Biblical Archaeologist* 47:3 [1984] 157).

8. Thus Richard Krautheimer interprets the phrase "breaking bread from house to house" in Acts 2:42 (Richard Krautheimer, *Early Christian and Byzantine Architecture*, 4th rev. ed., The Pelican History of Art [London: Penguin Books, 1986] 24).

9. See, for example, the illustrations in David Macaulay, *City: A Story of Roman Planning and Construction* (Boston: Houghton Mifflin Company, 1974) 71–75, 106–9.

10. Referring to Acts 16:13 and 19:9, Krautheimer writes, "Rarely would [Christians] be able to hire a public hall, as did the congregation at Ephesus at the time of St. Paul's visit" (Krautheimer, *Early Christian Architecture*, 24).

11. While it is true that residents of certain houses played key roles in the development of various local churches (for example, Prisca and Aquila, Acts 18:2-3 and 1 Cor 1:16), one cannot conclude that such homes were permanent places for the emerging Christian cult.

12. See Heb 3:6; 1 Pet 4:17; and 1 Tim 3:15; also, TDNT 5:121.

13. E.g., 1 Cor 10:16-17; 11:23-24.

14. Raymond Brown, *Priest and Bishop: Biblical Reflections* (New York: Paulist Press, 1970) 41–42.

15. Werner, "Jewish Music," NGDMM 9:625.

16. See the discussion of "The Jesus Experience" above (pp. 21–23).

17. "Hymn" is employed here with due caution. The next chapter will explore the various meanings and usages of this term. For now, it is sufficient to suggest that, in the present context, a hymn can be understood as any praise of God (or Christ) that employs what Josef Kroll calls "heightened speech"; see Josef Kroll, *Die Christliche Hymnodik bis zu Klemens von Alexandreia* (Königsberg im Br., 1921) 11.

18. These first four categories are borrowed from Reinhard Deichgräber, *Gotteshymnus und Christushymnus in der frühen Christenheit* (Göttingen: Vandenhoeck and Ruprecht, 1967).

19. Kroll contends that praise and thanks, much more than intercession, characterize the enthusiastic and spontaneous prayers of emerging Christianity (Kroll, *Christliche Hymnodik*, 11).

20. Deichgräber, *Gotteshymnus*, 24.

21. Anton Baumstark, *Comparative Liturgy*, rev. ed. (Westminster, Md.: Newman Press, 1958) 67.

22. For example, Werner, *Sacred Bridge*, 1:274; also, A. Hamman in *Early Christian Prayers*, trans. Walter Mitchell (London: Longmans, Green, 1961) 19.

23. Deichgräber, *Gotteshymnus*, 25.

24. Luke 2:14; Rom 11:36; 16:27; Eph 3:21; Phil 4:20; Gal 1:5; 1 Tim 1:17; 6:16; 2 Tim 4:18; 2 Cor 11:31; Heb 13:21; 1 Pet 4:11; 5:11; 2 Pet 3:18; Jude 25; Rev 1:6; 5:13; 7:10; 7:12; 19:1. For a further discussion of these passages and their doxological character, see my "The Question of Cultic Singing in the Christian Community of the First Century," unpublished M.A. thesis (University of Notre Dame, 1980) 70–74.

25. See Heinemann's discussion of *berakoth* in *Prayer in the Talmud*, 77–103.

26. Luke 1:68; Rom 1:25; 9:5; 2 Cor 1:3; 11:31; Eph 1:3; 1 Pet 1:3. For a further discussion of these New Testament *berakoth*, see my "The Question of Cultic Singing," 74–77.

27. Deichgräber, *Gotteshymnus*, 43.

28. 1 Cor 15:57; 2 Cor 2:14; 8:16; 9:15; Rom 6:17; 7:25; cf. 1 Tim 1:12; 1 Cor 1:14; 14:18.

29. Ralph P. Martin, *Carmen Christi: Philippians 2:5-11 in Recent Interpretation and in the Setting of Early Christian Worship* (Cambridge: Cambridge University Press, 1967) 19.

30. Werner, *Sacred Bridge*, 1:264.

31. Klaus-Peter Jörns, "Proklamation und Akklamation: Die antiphonische Grundordnung des frühchristlichen Gottesdienstes nach der Johannesoffenbarung," in Becker and Kaczynski, *Liturgie und Dichtung*, 1:187–208.

32. Rom 1:25; 9:5; 11:36; 16:27; Eph 3:21; Gal 1:5; Phil 4:20; 1 Tim 1:17; 6:16; 2 Tim 4:18; Heb 13:21; 1 Pet 4:11; 5:11; 2 Pet 3:18; Jude 25; Rev 1:5-6; 7:10, 12; 19:1.

33. Gal 6:18; Rev 1:7; 22:20.

34. Rev 19:1-6.

35. Mark 11:9-10; Matt 21:9, 15; John 12:3.

36. Eric Werner, "Hosanna in the Gospels," *Journal of Biblical Literature* 65 (1946) 103.

37. Joachim Jeremias, *The Prayers of Jesus* (Philadelphia: Fortress Press, 1978) 29.

38. Ibid., 34; also TDNT 1:6.

39. Rom 8:15 and Gal 4:6; for a further discussion of all these fragments and acclamations, see my "The Question of Cultic Singing," 79–90.

40. Raymond Brown, *The Birth of the Messiah* (Garden City, N.Y.: Doubleday and Company, 1977) 346.

41. Wilfred J. Harrington, *The Gospel According to St. Luke* (Westminster, Md.: Newman Press, 1967) 53.

42. Raymond Brown et al., *Mary in the New Testament* (Philadelphia: Fortress Press, 1978) 140 n. 311.

43. Brown, *The Birth of the Messiah*, 354; also, see Douglas Jones, "The Background and Character of the Lukan Psalms," *Journal of Theological Studies* 19 (1968) 47.

44. Brown, *The Birth of the Messiah*, 427.

45. Ibid.

46. Ibid.

47. Ibid., 350.

48. Three occur as introductory eulogies at the beginning of epistles (Eph 1:3-14; 1 Pet 1:3-5; 2 Cor 1:3-4), and a few others are simply two- or three-verse God-hymns (e.g., Rom 11:33-36; 1 Tim 6:15-16; Rev 15:3-4).

49. Deichgräber, *Gotteshymnus*, 60.

50. E.g., Acts 2:47; 3:8; 10:46; 11:18; 16:25; 21:20; 2 Cor 9:13; Gal 1:24; 1 Pet 2:12; Jas 3:9; Rev 15:6, 7. Joachim Gnilka concurs with this point, commenting on Ephesians 5:19: "To be sure, the thanks is ultimately directed to God, while the mediating place of Christ is clearly recognized" (Joachim Gnilka, "Der Christushymnus der Philipperbriefes [2,6-11] und die neutestamentliche Hymnendichtung," in Becker and Kaczynski, *Liturgie und Dichtung*, 1:174).

51. For an extended discussion of the various God-hymns in the New Testament, see my "The Question of Cultic Singing," 99–112.

52. Deichgräber, *Gotteshymnus*, 106; Jacques Schlosser mentions five other criteria for recognizing hymns in the New Testament: (1) a formal citation of the text, (2) poetic semblance ("l'allure poétique"), (3) style, especially the use of parallelisms and parataxis, (4) use of vocabulary that seems unfamiliar to the New Testament author or is especially expressive or rare, and (5) instances when the hymn "surpasses" ("le dépassement") or exceeds the argumentative or logical needs of the text (Jacques Schlosser, "Chants et hymnes dans le christianisme primitif," *Le Monde de la Bible* 37 [1985] 27–28).

53. Deichgräber designates Phil 2:6-11; 1 Tim 3:16; Heb 1:3; 1 Pet 2:21-24; and Col 1:15-20 (*Gotteshymnus*, 118–54). Martin, in *Carmen Christi*, lists Heb 1:3; Col 1:15-20; 1 Tim 3:16; John 1:1-14; 1 Pet 1:18-21; 2:21-25; 3:18-21; and Phil 2:6-11 (p. 19). Jack Sanders, in *The New Testament Christological Hymns* (Cambridge: Cambridge University Press, 1971), suggests Phil 2:6-11; Col 1:15-20; Eph 2:14-16; 1 Tim 3:16; 1 Pet 3:18-22; Heb 1:3; and John 1:1-14 (p. vii).

54. TDNT 8:500.

55. Gerhard Delling, *Worship in the New Testament*, trans. Percy Scott (Philadelphia: Westminster Press, 1962) 82, 87, and 88 respectively.

56. Paul Bradshaw, *Daily Prayer in the Early Church* (New York: Oxford University Press, 1982) 21.

57. The literature here is vast; apart from those sources already mentioned, a further sampling of opinions is found in Rudolph Bultmann, "Bekenntnis

und Liedfragmente im ersten Petrusbrief," *Exegetica* (1967) 285–97; Elizabeth Schüssler Fiorenza, "Wisdom Mythology and the Christological Hymns of the New Testament," in *Aspects of Wisdom in Judaism and Early Christianity*, ed. Robert Wilken (Notre Dame, Ind.: University of Notre Dame Press, 1975) 17–41; Gnilka, "Der Christushymnus der Philipperbriefes," 1:173–85; Robert Gundry, "The Form, Meaning and Background of the hymn quoted in 1 Tim. 3:16," in *Apostolic History and the Gospel*, Festschrift für F. F. Bruce (Exeter: Devon, 1970) 203–22; F. Manns, "Un hymne judéo-chrétien: Philippiens 2, 6-11," *Euntes Docete* 29 (1976) 259–90; J. M. Robinson, "Die Hodajot-Formel in Gebet und Hymnus des Frühchristentums," in *Apophoreta* Festschrift für Ernst Haenchen, ed. Walther Eltester and Franz Heinrich Kettler (Berlin: Topelmann, 1964) 194–235; and G. Wilhelmi, "Der Versöhnen-Hymnus in Eph. 2:14ff," *Zeitschrift für neutestamentliche Wissenschaft* 78 (1987) 145–52.

58. Joseph Gelineau, "Music and Singing in the Liturgy," in *The Study of Liturgy*, ed. Cheslyn Jones et al. (New York: Oxford University Press, 1978) 444.

59. The single Old Testament text that is cited the most in the New Testament is Psalm 110. See Gerhard Dautzenberg, "Psalm 110 im Neuen Testament," in Becker and Kaczynski, *Liturgie und Dichtung*, 1:141.

60. In the apocryphal Acts of Paul (ca. 190 C.E.) there is a reference to the "singing of David's psalms and hymns" (*Acta Pauli*, ed. and trans. Wilhelm Schubart and Carl Schmidt [Hamburg: J. J. Augustin, 1936] 50 and 51, line 11). The references to "psalms, hymns and spiritual songs" in Ephesians 5:19 and Colossians 3:16, while tantalizing, offer no precise distinction between these three genres, and offer no proof that the Davidic psalms were employed in early Christian worship; cf. TDNT 1:164.

61. Thus Bradshaw, for example, suggests that the "use of the Psalter may possibly have been in the formal services of the word and alongside non-canonical compositions at the agape" (Bradshaw, *Daily Prayer*, 45); also, Joseph Gelineau, "Les psaumes à l'époque patristique," *La Maison-Dieu* 135 (1978) 101.

62. See Mark 14:26 and Matthew 26:30; Joachim Jeremias, and others, accept this as a reference to the singing of the second half of the Passover Hallel (Pss 114 or 115 to 118). (Jeremias, *Eucharistic Words of Jesus*, 55).

63. See, for example, Thomas Talley, *The Origins of the Liturgical Year* (New York: Pueblo Books, 1986) 3–5.

64. See the discussion of "The Jesus Experience" above (pp. 21–23).

65. Luke 4:16-21.

66. Luke 24:13-35.

67. Justin Martyr, *First Apology* 67.3–8.

68. For example, there is reference to the public reading of letters in the congregation (2 Thess 5:27; Col 4:16), and to the cultic reading of the Old Testament (Luke 4:16; Acts 13:27; 15:21; 2 Cor 3:15; Rev 1:3).

69. Frederick Crowe, *Theology of the Christian Word* (New York: Paulist Press, 1978) 25.

70. TDNT 3:1107.

71. "The NT goes even farther than the Old in what it makes of the Word. . . . As is the case of no other religion, the Word is here the proper name of a person, the Son of God" (TDNT 3:1117).

72. Crowe, *Christian Word*, 22–42; Kittel concludes that since the word about Jesus is identical with Jesus himself, then what is said about Jesus can be said about the gospel: it is truth (2 Cor 4:2), a reliable word (1 Tim 1:15), and a two-edge sword (Heb 4:12), that demands a response and effects the promised salvation (TDNT 4:117).

73. Public "reading," as it developed in the early community, may not always have been an exact parallel to modern practice, especially in reference to the use of a book or written text. While there is great precedent for the use of scrolls, letters, and other written forms in the early Christian community, it is also possible—given the role of memory in this heightened auditory environment—that public "reading" consisted, for example, of a recitation of the sayings or parables of Jesus. This could have been especially true in that period before such saying were codified in written or gospel form.

74. See *Berakoth* 6.1–8.

75. The classic study is by Louis Finkelstein, "The Birkat Hamazzon," *Jewish Quarterly Review* 19 (1928–29) 211–63.

76. See, for example, Thomas Talley, "From Berakah to Eucharistia: A Reopening Question," *Worship* 50 (1976) 115–37; idem, "The Literary Structure of Eucharistic Prayer," *Worship* 58 (1984) 404–20.

77. 1 Corinthians 11 already attests to this process.

78. Beda Rigaux, *The Letters of St. Paul*, ed. and trans. Stephen Yonick (Chicago: Franciscan Herald Press, 1968) 132.

79. Luke 2:14; 2 Cor 11:31; Rev. 19:1.

80. Rom 1:25; 9:5.

81. E.g., Rom 7:25 and 2 Cor 9:15.

82. Delling, *Worship in the New Testament*, 64.

83. The congregational role was so important in the synagogue that the story is often recounted of the synagogue in Alexandria, where the size of the gathering made it difficult for the congregation to know when a benediction had ended. Thus, an official of the synagogue stood on the platform in the center of the synagogue and waved a handkerchief as a signal for the people to say their "amen" (*B. Sukkah* 51b).

84. See, for example, Fitzmyer, "Pauline Theology," NJBC 82:16.

85. The congregation responded with "halleluia" after each sentence of the Hallel psalms, according to Heinemann (*Prayer in the Talmud*, 145) and others.

86. "Halleluia" appears to function as a doxology in its only New Testament occurrence (Rev 19:1-6), as well as in the extra-biblical *Odes of Solomon*, in which "halleluia" concludes every ode. See *The Odes of Solomon*, ed. and trans. James H. Charlesworth (Missoula: University of Montana Press, 1977). Charlesworth suggests that the *Odes* are of Jewish-Christian origin, dating from very early; other scholars (e.g., W. Bauer, NTA 2:809) believe their time of com-

position to be comparable to that of the Book of Revelation or later.

87. For example, in *Didache* 10.6.

88. For the survey of opinions for and against the liturgical usage of each of the infancy canticles, God-hymns and Christological hymns noted above, see my "The Question of Cultic Singing," 90–122.

89. The Shema may have been performed in this way in some synagogues at the time of Jesus.

90. As previously noted, this is one accepted hypothesis for the performance of the *amidah* in the synagogues.

91. Jörns stresses that hearing or listening were never ends in themselves in early Christian worship, but had the purpose of calling forth the "amen" of the community, which was the true aim and symbol of the Spirit at work in the community (Jörns, "Proklamation und Akklamation," 1:193).

92. Avenary, "Music," EJ 12:578.

93. Commenting on Philippians 2:6-12, Werner notes:

> Another important factor in the formation and expansion of early Christian music was its Gentile wing, which brought the Palestinian-Syrian tradition into close contact with the Hellenized world. According to some scholars, the passage Phil 2:6-12 might perhaps be understood as a free poetic outburst. If their view is correct, we must consider it the first perceptible deviation from the spirit and structure of Hebrew poetry. There is no parallelism, not even a trace of lines similar to each other in length or in the number of accentuated syllables. If such a piece was ever sung, which is doubtful, it could not have been performed in the manner of traditional Jewish psalmody or like a canticle. (Werner, "Music," IDB 3:467).

94. These will be considered in the following section.

95. For a further discussion of these forms, see the discussion of "psalmody" above (pp. 52–53).

96. Avenary believes that a style of performing the psalms that can safely be ascribed to the first centuries C.E. entails "the sung recitation . . . generally on a single pitch, with melodic figures (cadences) attached to the middle and the end of the verse. Verses usually begin with an intonation motif. This modest configuration is repeated through the entire psalm; thus the music does not distract the listener's attention from the text" (Avenary, "Jewish Music," 1:955).

97. See Idelsohn, *Hebräisch-orientalischer Melodienschatz;* a sampling of these examples can be found in Idelsohn, *Jewish Music,* 62–64; also, Ergon Wellesz, *A History of Byzantine Music and Hymnography,* 2d ed. (Oxford: Clarendon Press, 1961) 35–37.

98. While it is not probable that all of these modes existed in the earliest stages of synagogue development, Idelsohn notes the eventual emergence of the following modes: the Pentateuch mode, the mode of Ruth, special modes for poetical portions of the Pentateuch, the prophetic mode, the mode of Lamentations, the mode of Job, various modes for the Psalms, and the mode of Esther.

For a further discussion of these various modes as well as musical illustrations, see Idelsohn, *Jewish Music*, 39–66.

99. "Psalmody and melodic reading are common traits of all the 'peoples of the bible.' Repeated attempts to find an archetype of it in pagan antiquity have not succeeded" (Avenary, "Music," EJ 12:578).

100. "Plain recitation (spoken), ecphonesis (*Sprechgesang*, or a semi-musical recitative) and cantillation (regular musical chant)" (Werner, *Sacred Bridge*, 1:104).

101. Thus Werner concludes, "It is not possible to compare simply Jewish and Christian practices concerning the chant of the lesson. Here the respective traditions are too incommensurate: while Judaism has established a minutely elaborated system of ecphonetic accents applied to every word, the Churches have limited themselves mostly to closing or pausal accents of verses" (Werner, *Sacred Bridge*, 1:456).

102. See Eric Werner's comments on the musical influence of the "Gentile wing" in the formation and expansion of early Christian music (above, note 93). One caution in attempting to assess the influence of the various musical traditions of Gentile believers on emerging Christian worship is that Judaism at the time of Jesus was already a Hellenized Judaism, clearly influenced by Greek culture (see, for example, Martin Hengel, *Judaism and Hellenism: Studies in Their Encounter in Palestine during the Early Hellenistic Period*, trans. John Bowden [Philadelphia: Fortress Press, 1975]; also, idem., *The 'Hellenization' of Judaea in the First Century after Christ*, trans. John Bowden [London: SCM Press, 1989]). The growing dominance of Gentile Christians, however, must have significantly magnified such Hellenizing influences.

103. That is, in the setting of an extended family where there was a natural and ordinary leader: the head of the household.

104. What existed was not so much a text as a formula that was improvised by the head of the household in three stanzas or on three separate themes, each of which probably concluded with a doxology-type refrain by the gathered family.

105. See Talley, "From Berakah to Eucharistia," esp. 89–92.

106. Avenary, "Music," EJ 12:578.

107. E.g., cymbals (1 Cor 13:1), gongs (1 Cor 13:1), pipes (Matt 9:23; 11:17; Luke 7:32; 1 Cor 14:7; Rev 18:22), trumpets (1 Cor 14:8), *shofars* (Rev 8:2, 6, 12; 9:1-13), harps (Rev 5:8; 14:2; 15:2).

108. Johannes Quasten, *Music and Worship in Pagan and Christian Antiquity*, trans. Boniface Ramsey (Washington: Pastoral Press, 1983 [1973]) 72–73.

109. Werner, "Music," IDB 3:466.

110. James McKinnon, *Current Musicology* 1 (1985) 74–75; McKinnon spins out his complete argument in "The Church Fathers and Musical Instruments" (Ph.D. dissertation, Columbia University, 1962).

111. Werner, *Sacred Bridge*, 2:149–75.

112. E.g., the spiritualization of the Temple sacrifice, the spiritualization of the meal, etc.; see Finkelstein's discussion of such spiritualization in terms of the *Didache* ("The Birkat Hamazzon," 214).

113. "Since the early Christians improvised much of their chant, it is possible to postulate the influence of the folk music of the Hellenized Syrian littoral (i.e. music neither learned nor popular; the music of the taverns and markets). Modern religious music suggests this by analogy" (Christian Hannick, "Christian Music," NGDMM 4:365).

114. See Jörns, "Proklamation und Akklamation," passim.

115. I.e., "glossolalia," mentioned in 1 Corinthians 14, which is quite different from the foreign languages of Acts 2:4-11. See the discussion in Jerome Murphy-O'Connor's commentary on "The First Letter to the Corinthians," NJBC 49:63-64; also, Johannes Behm's article on "glossa," TDNT 1:722-26.

5 The Era of the House Church (Second and Third Centuries C.E.)

The Setting

What is notable in the era of the house church is not that Christians gathered in domestic dwellings, for that was something they did from the inception of the Jesus movement. What is notable is that eventually specific houses were acquired and set aside for cultic use. At the beginning of the movement, borrowed rooms and the homes of believers were important gathering places. With the destruction of the Temple and the separation of the Christian community from the synagogue, these domestic settings became virtually the only place for community worship.[1]

It is difficult to generalize about the types of homes that existed in the Roman Empire during the first centuries of the common era.[2] It was not uncommon to find large, four-sided structures for the wealthy in the urban centers of the empire. The normal inclusion of a large dining room well suited for Eucharist as well as a pool in the atrium adaptable for baptism made them very serviceable buildings. Structurally these houses faced inward with open spaces at the center. The resulting walled-off interior provided shelter from the commotion of the street and the disapproving gaze of pagan neighbors and authorities.[3]

Homes for the lower or middle class were quite different. In the Eastern provinces, according to Krautheimer, there were single-family dwellings up to four storeys high. The only large room was the dining room on the top floor, which often opened on to a terrace. Krautheimer imagines that it was such a dwelling, with the congregation crowded into the upper room, that served as the setting for the incident at Troas during which a young man, apparently dozing on the window sill, fell to the ground and was raised from the dead by Paul (Acts 20:7-12).[4] In Rome, tenement houses with horizontal apartments were the rule. Some of these apartments may not have included a dining room, so the community used any available room of appropriate size for their gatherings.[5]

Krautheimer believes that before 200 C.E., Christian congregations were restricted to these ''inconspicuous dwellings of the lower class.''[6] Murphy-O'Connor, on the other hand, suggests that even in the first century, the Christian community gathered (although not exclusively) in the homes of wealthy believers[7]—the precedent for which can be found in the ministry of Jesus himself.[8]

In the early history of these domestic gatherings one can imagine the worshipping community respecting the limitations of another family's dwelling. Permanent changes in the structure would have been inappropriate. The community likely rearranged furniture in order to accommodate its worship. In the dining room, or some other large gathering space, a single table could have been used for Eucharist with a chair for the host or bishop who led the worship. As the size of the community increased and the limits of ordinary rooms were tested it is possible that a community looked for larger homes in which to gather.

Eventually communities sought permanent homes for worship and other gatherings. It is impossible to say for certain when this first occurred. It is generally true that homes provided the setting for Christian worship until the dawn of the fourth century C.E. If, however, Krautheimer means to suggest that prior to 200 C.E. Christians did not own any domestic buildings or set such buildings aside exclusively for ecclesial use, his hypothesis can be argued only from silence.

The clearest ancient archaeological evidence of a Christian ''housechurch'' is that of Dura-Europos.[9] Destroyed in 257, the building dates from around 230, and seems to have been structurally altered to suit the needs of the Christian community, which was in possession of the structure, between 240 and 250.[10] Literary evidence from various other places of the time confirm that other communities also had their own buildings.[11]

The reasons why Christians found it important or even necessary to establish permanent settings for their gatherings are multiple and complex. Contributing factors include the rapid growth of the Christian community,[12] the increased complexification of the cult

FIGURE 4. HOUSE CHURCH AT DURA EUROPOS
Plan of the house church at Dura Europos after Peter Cobb, ''The Architectural Setting of the Liturgy'' in *The Study of the Liturgy,* ed. Cheslyn Jones *et al.* (Oxford University Press, New York, 1978) p. 481.

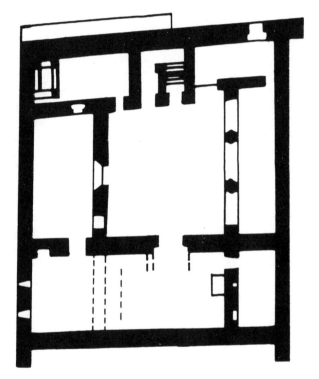

with commensurate demands upon the worship space,[13] and widespread toleration of Christians in and outside of the empire.[14] White believes that one can document the emergence of a more distinctively Christian material culture between the time of Justin Martyr (d. ca. 165) and the *Constitutio Antoniana* (212), which conferred citizenship upon all free inhabitants of the empire.[15] These and other factors testify to Christianity's transition from the status of sect and movement to that of a full-scale religion.

Beyond these measurable factors, Kelber's reflections on the rise of the written gospel might offer a further insight into why permanent domestic churches developed within Christianity. Kelber suggests that the development of the written gospel within the Christian community must not be seen as a natural, evolutionary progression from oral to written forms but as a radical change.[16] Oral forms, in Kelber's view, support images of the heroic and dynamic, whereas written forms give people the distance necessary to reassess and more completely appreciate the experience of the heroic. In specific reference to the Jesus experience, Kelber summarizes, "It may thus not be an exaggeration to claim that it was with Mark's extraordinary narrative that Christian consciousness was jolted out of oral infancy and partial amnesia of Jesus' death toward a fully historicized grasp of the life and death of the messiah."[17]

Could not something similar be said of permanent ecclesial settings vis-à-vis borrowed spaces in early Christianity? The former may not have been so much a natural evolution from the latter, but a counterreform. The growth in the number of believers, their increased visibility and acceptance, their gradual abandonment of itinerant leadership and growing reliance on resident *episcopoi*[18] and their image of themselves (i.e., not so much as a sect or even a local religion, but as a belief system and church that spanned the empire) called forth a radically different setting for their cult. In some respects, like the rise of the written gospel, the emergence of the permanent house church marked the end of an heroic era and enabled the community to move toward a fully historicized grasp of the life and death of the Messiah.

Emerging Christian "Musicians"

Unlike the previous era, this period does offer ample witness to the singing of the Davidic psalms in various Christian gatherings. What it does not yield, however, is any evidence of a psalmist, cantor, or any other person who might be considered a permanent or official musician in the Christian community.

This is somewhat striking since literary sources from the period testify to the existence of numerous other liturgical ministers and officials. Hippolytus (d. ca. 236), for example, notes that there were deacons, subdeacons, and readers;[19] Cornelius of Rome (d. 253) in his letter of 251 to Fabius attests to the presence of acolytes, exorcists, and doorkeepers;[20] the *Didaskalia* (ca. 225) knows of deaconesses;[21] and Tertullian (d. ca. 225) considers widows to be part of the clergy.[22] Yet in none of these listings, church orders, or correspondence do we hear of a singer, psalmist, or cantor.[23]

One exception could be an epitaph from Hadrian in Bythinia which H. Leclercq claims is "certainly anterior to the peace of the Church, probably appearing in the second or third century."[24] The epitaph commemorates an eighteen-year-old man who was known for "chanting the praises of the most high, and training all the faithful to chant the sacred psalms and the reading of the holy books."[25] If this epitaph originated in the second or third century it could be our earliest known reference to someone leading the assembly in psalm singing.

Leclercq's contention that this "young cantor held the office of psaltes and anagnostes,"[26] however, is overdrawn. The epitaph speaks of no office but only of action, not of a "chanter" but of "chanting." Furthermore, the epitaph attests to the intimate relationship between singing and reading, between psalms and lections; not, as Leclercq suggests, because in this era there was "not always sufficient hierarchical personnel to fulfill the diverse functions of the church,"[27] but because the community as yet saw little distinction between the sung and the publicly spoken. As such a division between singers and speakers, or between cantors and readers, was unnecessary at that time, so "reader" was the only designation given to those responsible for cantillation, be it of psalms or lessons.[28]

Christian "Song"

During this period the previously discussed forms from the New Testament, readings, and anaphora continued to exist as lyrical elements of the worship. Since these would have functioned virtually the same as in the previous era, we will not give them specific attention here. Rather, we will focus on the psalms of David, "hymnodic psalmody," and metrical hymns.

Psalms

Prior to the third century of the common era there is little explicit evidence that the Davidic psalms were anything like a "songbook" for the early Christian community. This has led some, like Balthasar Fischer, to suggest that the Old Testament psalms were never a part of Christian cult during the first two centuries.[29] Fischer argues that the early Church only turned to the Psalter as a songbook in response to questionable hymn texts that were "radically compromised by gnostic abuses." He concludes that the trend toward accepting the Psalter in Christian worship occurred only around 200 C.E.

It is true that, along with the previously noted apocryphal *Acts of Paul,* the earliest clear evidence for psalms in Christian worship clusters around the year 200.[30] Evidence before this time is fragmentary and ambiguous. As previously noted, it is possible that the psalms served as a book of readings for the early Christian community;[31] that psalm fragments might have found their way into preaching or proclamation; that new psalm-like compositions emerged; and that traditional biblical psalms were reinterpreted in light of the Jesus experience. It is not possible, however, to ascertain any set pattern for employing psalms within Christian worship of the first century. What is new in the third century, therefore, is not so much that psalms are employed for the first time in Christian worship, but that patterns for their usage develop and clarify. Tertullian, for example, indicates that psalm-singing is an ordinary element of the "liturgy of the word" for the Sunday assembly.[32]

As to why psalmody became a constitutive element of Christian worship after the third century, one can only surmise. Fischer's suggestion that the biblical psalms were an appropriate and effective "antidote" to more contemporary compositions of questionable content certainly could have been one reason. Another is what Werner characterizes as a trend from spontaneous to more organized patterns of prayer.[33] It is around the year 200, for example, that the New Testament canon began to be defined[34] and the first written model for a Eucharistic Prayer appeared.[35] This general move toward standardization in creedal and prayer formulae could have been the impetus for the further standardization of Christian worship. The adoption of the Davidic psalms was one more step in this process.

Hymnodic Psalmody

We have already employed the term *hymn* as a designation for certain larger lyrical forms in the New Testament, such as God-hymns and Christological hymns.[36] Such works were largely "poetical-prose"[37] compositions of uneven meter and stress[38] constructed in imitation of biblical patterns like the Davidic psalms.[39] Cattin and others call such works "hymnodic psalmody"[40] to distinguish them from the metrical and strophic structures that were to arise later. It is possible that this is the lyric genre that lies behind Pliny's allusive reference to believers chanting[41] "a hymn to Christ as to a God" in his letter to Trajan (ca. 112 C.E.).[42]

One extant collection of Christian hymnodic psalmody is the *Odes of Solomon*. This collection of forty-two odes was probably the work of Jewish Christians in Palestine in the late first century C.E.[43] Written in imitation of the Davidic psalms, these *psalmi idiotici* employ a parallel structure in which each verse is divided in half (a colon) by a caesura (or sentence-stop)[44]—a Semiticism captured in Charlesworth's translation of *Ode* 1:

1. The Lord is on my head like a crown,
   And I shall never be without him.

2. Plaited for me is the crown of truth
   And it caused Thy branches to blossom in me.

3. For it is not like a parched crown that blossoms not;

4. But thou livest upon my head,
   And have blossomed upon me.

5. Thy fruits are full and complete;
   They are full of Thy salvation.

Other hymnodic psalms can be found in such apocryphal acts as those of John[45] and Thomas.[46] According to Wellesz, although these works are transmitted in Greek, the language demonstrates many characteristics of Semitic poetry.[47] The works of certain gnostic writers can also be considered hymnodic psalms.[48] Important here is Bar-Daisan (d. 222) who, with his son Harmonius, composed a new psalter.[49] As for orthodox writers, Kroll would argue for the existence of "hymns" in the works of Ignatius of Antioch (d. ca. 107) and Melito of Sardis (d. ca. 190).[50]

A further stage in the evolution of this genre is evident in the third-century hymn "Phos Hilaron." No longer a binary structure of parallel half-verses with a break in the middle, this Greek text is composed of three strophes, each of which contains four lines.[51] Despite this structural development, "Phos Hilaron" must still be considered a piece of "poetical-prose,"[52] as it lacks the alternation of long and short syllables as well as the regular distribution of stresses that characterizes classical poetry and would characterize later Christian hymnody. This is true of a number of other Greek poetical-prose compositions from the early Christian centuries.[53]

At the beginning of the third century Tertullian noted the existence of hymnody among the heretics. Jacques Fontaine believes this to be an important reference, bolstering the hypothesis that heretics were the first to employ "hymns" on a regular basis.[54] Tertullian's information about worship in his own community[55] suggests that, in Africa at the beginning of the third century, there existed charismatic hymnody, individually improvised and yet demonstrating a certain concurrence between biblical canticles and the new improvisations.[56] The continuity between these forms and the possible reliance of new improvisations upon biblical prototypes suggest, again, that the type of hymnody under discussion is really hymnodic psalmody.

Metrical Hymnody

While Judaism provided the models for the development of hymnodic psalmody in emerging Christianity, it was the classical poetry of the Greco-Roman world that provided models for the emergence of metrical hymnody. Here the central organizing principle was meter which, although present in biblical poetry and later works written in imitation of biblical poetry, was not their basic organizing principle.[57]

Christian acquaintance with classical poetry may be detectable as early as Paul who, in his discourse to the Athenians (Acts 17:16ff.), seems to refer to two poetic Greek texts: the "Phaenomena" of Aratus of Soli (d. ca. 239 B.C.E.), and the "Hymn to Zeus" by Cleanthes (d. ca. 232 B.C.E.).[58] This acquaintance did not translate into early acceptance. The first extant example of an orthodox Christian hymn composed in classical meter is the sixty-five short line, anapaest work of Clement of Alexandria (d. 215).[59] It is quite probable that Clement was imitating a style of metrical poetry that was adopted earlier by gnostic believers.[60] Wellesz contends that such hymns "represent an attempt by educated men to preserve Greek civilization," and that Clement's hymn of praise to Christ "shows how the master of the Catechetical school tried to combine the spirit of Greek poetry with Christian theology."[61] A few lines from Clement's hymn, even in translation, make the point:

> King of Saints, Almighty Word
> of the Father, Highest Lord,
>
> Wisdom's head and chief
> Assuagement of all grief;
>
> Lord of all time and space
> Jesus, Saviour of our Race.[62]

There is considerable disagreement over whether or not this hymn was ever employed in worship.[63] Nevertheless, this work does attest to the emergence of a style of Christian hymnody that is not exclusively or essentially dependent upon Semitic prototypes, but finds its roots in classical Greek forms. From this experiment will develop works most accurately described as Christian hymns, that is, new works of metrical[64] poetry, in which the texts come to be structured into stanzas of two or more lines, with each stanza employing the same meter and number of lines.

Clement's testimony in the East has some parallels in the West. Fontaine suggests that, little by little, there is a "thaw" in Western Christianity's opposition toward pagan poetry, beginning in the third century.[65] This is evident in the *Octavius* of Minucius Felix (d. ca. 220), where there is great reverence for the work and 'theology" of Virgil, as well as in the work of Arnobius (d. ca. 330) and his pupil Lactantius (d. ca. 320). At the same time, Christian leaders became increasingly critical of pagan music practices. As McKinnon summarizes,

> The first hint of the polemic against pagan music appeared in the work of the late second-century converted rhetorician Tatian, who wrote: "I do not wish to gape at many singers, nor do I care to look benignly upon a man who is nodding and motioning in an unnatural way." The polemic grew in explicitness and intensity throughout the third

century, particularly with Latin Africans like Tertullian and Arnobius, and became a commonplace among the major figures of the fourth like John Chrysostom, Ambrose and Augustine.[66]

This paradoxical confluence of adaptation and critique will contribute to the first golden age of Christian hymnody, represented by Hilary of Poitiers (d. 367) and Ambrose (d. 397) in the West, and Ephraem the Syrian (d. 373) in the East.

The Oxyrhynchus Hymn

Along with all of the literary, epitaphic, and iconographic monuments to Christian music in the first three centuries, there is one musical fragment that survives from this formative period of Christianity. The Oxyrhynchus hymn takes its name from Oxyrhynchus (Bahnasa), an archaeological site in Egypt[67] where many thousands of Greek, Latin, Coptic, and Arabic documents were discovered between 1897 and 1907.[68] Papyrus 1786 in this collection contains the closing words and music of a hymn to the Trinity[69] dating from the end of the third century.[70] The text is in Greek and notated in what is sometimes called classical Greek vocal notation. While there is much unanimity when it comes to transcribing the hymn,[71] which many agree to have been based on a diatonic Hypolydian scale, there is much disagreement concerning the relationship of the hymn to classical Greek music,[72] and the proper manner of its performance.[73] One further wonders to what extend this singular monument—which may or may not have been employed in worship—is typical of Christian music at any stage of its development.

"Song" Forms

Apart from the Oxyrhynchus fragment, none of the monuments of Christian music in this era provide sufficient information to allow for the melodic reconstruction of early Christian music. Consequently, in this section we will concentrate more on the forms of the music, and offer an occasional reflection about melodic or rhythmic elements. Since this has already been done for the Oxyrhynchus hymn in the previous section, it will not be treated separately below.

Psalms

The increased information about the employment of the Davidic psalms in this period allows more clarity as to the performance of these psalms in the Christian cult. Tertullian, for example, notes that when Christians gather for common prayer, "The more diligent in prayer are accustomed to add in their prayers the 'halleluia' and such kind of psalms at the close of which the company may respond."[74] This reference suggests that the community knew responsorial forms in which "alleluia or some other responsory as part of the text itself . . . were chosen so that the company could respond at the end of the verses."[75] Evidence for responding to psalms with "alleluia," already a part of Jewish practice, is clear in the second and third centuries of the Christian era.[76]

Evidence that the community responded to a psalm with more than a single word is sketchy in this period. An examination of the literature has led E. T. Moneta Caglio to conclude that responsorial psalmody did not exist in the East much before the end of the third century[77] and that Ambrose introduced responsorial psalmody into the West, in imitation of the Eastern practice.[78] Such a conclusion, however, seems to draw too sharp a distinction between responsorial forms that employed only a single word (e.g., "alleluia") and those that employed phrases, half verses, or full verses as the response. Furthermore, as Cattin suggests, "the global scale of subsequent developments is such that the argument [against the existence of the responsorial psalm before the third century] *e silentio* seems very weak, the more so because the Biblical precedents for psalms with a refrain are particularly notable . . . even if their plan is not exactly that of the Christian responsorial psalm."[79]

Besides these responsorial variations,[80] it is also probable that this epoch knew both solo psalmody and unison[81] performance of psalms. Evidence for the former can be found in Tertullian: "Each is asked to step forward and sing, according to his ability, a hymn to God, either from the Holy Scriptures or his own composition."[82] Although "hymn . . . from the Holy Scriptures" could refer to some non-psalmic song from the Hebrew Bible or a New Testament canticle, it is also quite probable that Tertullian is referring to psalm-singing here, especially given the other notable references to psalm-singing in his works. Evidence for unison congregational psalm-singing is rooted in the patristic notion of "singing with one voice."[83] Ignatius of Antioch (d. 107) is often cited as the classical patristic

101

source for such thinking.[84] Clement of Alexandria specifically speaks of psalm-singing in this mode: "It is fitting to bless the Maker of all things before we partake of food; so, too, at a feast, when we enjoy his created gifts, it is only right that we sing psalms to him. In fact, a psalm sung in unison is a blessing, and it is an act of self-restraint."[85] There appears to be no evidence from this period for alternating or antiphonal psalmody.[86]

Hymnodic Psalmody

The wide range of forms that emerged in imitation of Davidic psalmody called forth an equally wide range of performance styles. The *Odes of Solomon,* for example, with their recurring "alleluia" refrain suggest a performance style akin to that of the alleluiac psalms, in which the assembly punctuated a solo performance with "alleluia" or some other such refrain.[87] The previously cited reference from Tertullian[88] attests to the existence of solo (improvised) *psalmi idiotici* in the early patristic period. Finally, the strophic construction of a prose hymn such as "Phos Hilaron" suggests that the Christian community of this era also had in their repertoire prose compositions that were performed in unison by a group or the entire assembly. While there is less explicit evidence to prove that the hymnodic psalmody of the early Christian community was performed responsorially, the previously postulated ubiquitous presence of this form in emerging Christianity makes it difficult to refute out of hand its employment with hymnodic psalms.[89]

As to the sound of such performances, one can only hypothesize. It is probable that the forms more closely allied with Davidic psalmody relied on similar music.[90] The emergence of new hybrids, like "Phos Hilaron," undoubtedly stretched the musical vocabulary of the early Christian community.[91]

Metrical Hymnody

A central characteristic of emerging Christian metrical hymnody was a text of metrical poetry, structured into stanzas of two or more lines, with each stanza employing the same meter and number of lines. Such hymns could have been performed by soloists or even small groups.[92] It is also possible that they were performed responsorially, with the leader singing each line and the assembly repeating it. The repetition of poetic and melodic units, characteristic of this structure, also suggests that such hymns were sung by an assembly without any division in the text. The common singing of hymns by the whole assembly could also be suggested by the previously noted concern for "singing with one voice" as well as the universal tradition, in the ancient Greek-speaking world, of choruses singing in unison.[93]

Attempting to imagine the sound of such hymns is difficult. Hannick's summary is clear and typical: "Although the texts of some Christian hymns are known, their melodic structure is not. Even the Oxyrhynchus fragment containing musical notation . . . cannot serve as a basis for investigation, and the evidence of the Fathers is inconclusive."[94] One tantalizing but inconclusive piece of evidence from the Fathers is the complaint Clement of Alexandria registers against the use of chromaticisms.[95]

Instruments

The previous summary on the use and place of instruments in the emerging Christian cult applies to this period as well. Although the literature expands, and references to musical instruments abound,[96] instruments still played no significant role in the Christian worship of this era. The reasons for this are as complex as those for the previous era. Emphasis on the primacy of vocal music and a concern of Christians to distinguish their worship practices from those of pagans certainly helped to shape worship without instruments—a tradition that would flourish for more than a millennium.

Summary on "Christian Music" of the Second and Third Centuries

In some respects, the musical developments of this era are symbolic of the basic evolution of the Christian community in the second and third centuries after the death of Christ. It was during this time that Christianity emerged as a recognizable religion, with a distinctive cult, forms of ministry, places of worship, scriptural canon, and literature. While still indebted to Judaism, it had clearly separated from Judaism, confronted the Greco-Roman world and gained recognition as a distinctive group by that world.[97]

Similar things could be said about its music. It was in this period that identifiable Christian musical forms developed. While closely connected to the lyricism of the previous age, this "music" was distinctive in text and tone. The debt to Judaism was still evident in the general absence of instruments, the plethora of *psalmi idiotici* composed in this era, and the patterned borrowing of the Davidic psalms. A new alliance with Greco-Roman culture, however, shows itself in the development of metrical hymnody and poetic texts.

The spirit of the primitive community does not seem to be compromised by this new cultural alliance. The acoustic environment suggests that there was still no sharp distinction between the sung and the spoken, no clear division between what we might call the musical and the non-musical, nor any denial of the fundamental lyricism of Christian worship. It is, therefore, still difficult to consider music a separate element in the Christian cult at this time. Rather, it was the aural aspect of that cult. This perspective is further reflected in the total absence of any references to special singers, psalmists, or cantors. There is no separate liturgical musician. The whole of worship is musical, and to the extent that the worship belonged to the whole assembly, so did the music belong to them.

NOTES FOR CHAPTER FIVE

1. Exceptions to this can be found, for example, in the apocryphal *Acts of Paul* 11.

2. As White notes, "House patternings varied considerably across the empire: the Italian villa, the Greek peristyle, the Hellenistic-oriental multistoried insula, apartments, and others had their own local stylistic traditions. We must expect, then, that . . . there was considerable diversity from place to place depending on the local circumstances of each cell group" (White, *Building God's House,* 107).

3. Macauley provides a splendid introduction to such homes in *City,* 66–70; for a more scholarly introduction, see Alexander McKay, *Houses, Villas and Palaces in the Roman World* (Ithaca: Cornell University Press, 1975).

4. Krautheimer, *Early Christian Architecture,* 24.

5. Ibid.

6. Ibid., also 456, n. 24; the reasoning outlined in the latter is faulty, for it presumes that, for example, gardens and audience halls could not have been used by the early Christian community because they would have been "utterly unsuitable for the ritual meals of the believers." What Krautheimer fails to note

is that the meal is one of the first elements to drop out of the emerging Christian cult, and Paul in his First Letter to the Corinthians already announces its absence.

7. Murphy-O'Connor, "The Corinth That Saint Paul Saw," 157; idem, *St. Paul's Corinth: Texts and Archaeology* (Wilmington: Michael Glazier, 1983 [Collegeville: The Liturgical Press, 1990]) 153–61.

8. For example, the Lukan account of Jesus dining with Simon the Pharisee (7:39-50) and Zaccheus the chief tax collector (19:1-10), and Mark's account of Jesus entering the house of Jairus, the synagogue official (5:35-43).

9. The literature on this excavation is vast. For an introduction to the church, see Krautheimer, *Early Christian Architecture*, 27; for a more general introduction to the excavation, see Clark Hopkins, *The Discovery of Dura-Europos* (New Haven: Yale University Press, 1979); the classic study on the church is C. H. Kraeling, *The Christian Building: The Excavations at Dura Europos Conducted by Yale University and the French Academy of Inscriptions and Letters: Final Report 8:2* (New Haven: Yale University Press, 1967).

10. Krautheimer, *Early Christian Architecture*, 27. On the issue of adaptation or renovation as a transitional stage of early Christian architecture, see White, *Building God's House*, 21–22.

11. The emperor Severus Augustus (d. 235), for example, allowed Christians to purchase a public property (The Writers of Augustan History: *Severus Alexander* 49.6).

12. According to Adolph von Harnack, for example, there could have been as many as fifty thousand Christians in Rome by 250 (Adolph von Harnack, *The Mission and Expansion of Christianity in the First Three Centuries*, trans. James Moffatt, 2d rev. ed. [London: Williams and Norgate, 1908] 247).

13. The *Didaskalia Apostolorum* (early third century), for example, offers a relatively detailed instruction for the physical disposition of the community during worship (12).

14. Persecutions of Christians were usually short-lived and confined to specific locations: for example, under Nero (d. 68 C.E.) in Rome, Domitian (d. ca. 96) in Rome, Trajan (d. 117) in Asia Minor, Marcus Aurelius (d. 180) in Lyons, and Decius (d. 251) and Diocletian (d. 305) throughout the empire.

15. White, *Building God's House*, 118; in support of this claim he cites Graydon Snyder who considers the period between 180 and 200 as the time during which "Christian art, funerary symbolism, and the building began to achieve their own cultural definition" (Graydon Snyder, *Ante Pacem: Archaeological Evidence of Church Life Before Constantine* [Macon, Ga.: Mercer, 1985] 163–65, as cited in White, *Building God's House*, 118).

16. Kelber, *The Oral and the Written Gospel*, 209.

17. Ibid., 211.

18. See, for example, Nathan Mitchell, *Mission and Ministry*, Message of the Sacraments 6 (Wilmington: Michael Glazier, 1982 [Collegeville: The Liturgical Press, 1990]) 137–200.

19. Hippolytus, *Apostolic Tradition* 4.

20. This letter is recorded in Eusebius, *The History of the Church*, 6.43.

21. *Didaskalia* 2.26.6.

22. Tertullian, *On Monogamy* 11.1.

23. For a survey of the documentary evidence for singers in the early Church, see Brian Joseph Sparksman, "The Minister of Music in the Western Church: A Canonical-Historical Survey," unpublished J.C.D. dissertation (The Catholic University of America, 1980), especially the first two chapters.

24. H. Leclercq, "Chantres," *Dictionnaire d'Archéologie Chrétienne et de Liturgie* 3 (1914) 345.

25. Ibid.

26. Ibid.

27. Ibid.

28. *The Apostolic Constitutions* (ca. 380 C.E.) seems to be breaking new ground when it indicates that someone besides the reader of the lessons should sing the psalms (2.57.6).

29. Balthasar Fischer, "Le Christ dans les psaumes," *La Maison-Dieu* 27 (1951) 86–113.

30. For example, possibly Clement of Alexandria (d. 215), *Stromata* 7.7.49; Hippolytus, *Apostolic Tradition* ch. 25 (ca. 215 C.E.); the *Didascalia Apostolorum* (ca. 225 C.E.) 6.5; Tertullian, *On the Flesh of Christ* 20.3.

31. That the Book of Psalms continued to be considered a prophetic book and was, therefore, possibly read as such in early Christian worship is supported, for example, by the writings of Justin Martyr (d. ca. 165) who includes quotes from the psalms in his discussion of the Hebrew prophets who foretold the coming of Christ (e.g., Justin Martyr, *Apology* 1.31–41).

32. "The Scriptures are read, psalms are sung, sermons are delivered and petitions are offered" (Tertullian, *On the Soul* 9); for a general discussion of the role of psalmody in the liturgy as reflected in the writings of Tertullian, see E. Dekkers, *Tertullianus en de geschiedenis der Liturgie* (Brussels and Amsterdam: Desclée de Brouwer, 1947) 31–36.

33. Werner, "Music," IDB 3:467.

34. "In the East Clement of Alexandria and in the West Tertullian were developing the basic language of the two Testaments. In the same general period, the Muratorian Fragment and Origen gave lists of NT books—a sign that the concept of a collection of Christian Scriptures had taken hold" (NJBC 66:81).

35. Hippolytus, *Apostolic Tradition* 4.

36. In attempting to discern what might be considered an early Christian hymn, Ralph Martin offers the following direction:

> There are no metrical standards available at this point in the development of Christian worship. Metrical verses came later; and it is only in the third century that we have examples of anapaestic metre and musical notation. The criteria which are available are stylistic tests, of which the most obvious traits are: a certain rhythmical lilt ascertainable when

the passage is read aloud, a correspondence between words and phrases which are placed in the sentences in an obviously carefully selected position, not always ad sensum; the use of parallelismus membrorum (i.e. an arrangement into couplets); and traces of a rudimentary metre and the employment of rhetorical devices such as homoeoteleuton, alliteration, antithesis and chiasmus'' (Martin, *Carmen Christi*, 12–13).

37. A term of Egon Wellesz that respects the fact that these are ''poetic'' works that have a strong affinity with prose forms (Wellesz, *A History of Byzantine Music and Hymnography*, 149). The border between prose and poetry was often blurred in ''hymns'' from the classical world at time as well, e.g., those of Pliny the Elder (d. 79 C.E.), and Apuleius (d. ca. 123 C.E.) Wünsch, ''Hymos,'' *Paulys Real-Encyclopädie der classischen Altertums Wissenschaft*, ed. Wilhelm Kroll [Stuttgart: J. B. Metzler, 1914] 19/1:180).

38. Anton Baumstark calls these ''prose hymns'' (Anton Baumstark, ''Hymns [Greek Christian],'' *Encyclopaedia of Religion and Ethics*, ed. James Hastings [New York: Scribner's Sons, 1915] 7:5 and passim).

39. For a further description of the structure of Hebrew psalmody, see Corbin, *L'église à la conquête de sa musique*, 132.

40. Cattin, *Music of the Middle Ages 1*, 18; Kroll uses the term ''prose-hymn'' [*Prosahymnus*] (Kroll, *Christiliche Hymnodik*, 8).

41. ''Carmen dicere'' may mean to ''sing'' or ''chant'' a hymn: a reading enhanced by Tertullian's *Apology* 2.6, which quotes this passage from Pliny, and ''definitely understands carmen dicere in the sense of canere'' (Willi Rordorf, *Sunday*, trans. A. K. Graham [London: SCM Press, LTD, 1968] 259 n. 3).

42. ''Carmen Christo quasi deo dicere secum invicem'' (Pliny, *Letter* 10.96); see Ralph Martin, ''A Footnote to Pliny's Account of Christian Worship,'' in *Vox Evangelica 3*, ed. Ralph Martin (London: Epworth Press, 1964) 51–57; a more recent survey of opinion on this passage can be found in Jorg Christian Salzmann, ''Pliny (Ep. 10.96) and Christian Liturgy—a Reconsideration,'' *Studia Patristica* 20 (1989) 389–95.

43. Charlesworth, *The Odes of Solomon*, 90, 113, and passim.

44. ''The biblical [poetic] line consists of two balanced cola. The balance between them can be metrical (the roughly equal length of the cola), syntactic, morphological, phonic, semantic, and of other types too disparate to catalogue here. Every line has approximate metrical balance. In all of the other areas the balance can run from nothing or next to nothing, to moderate to extreme. . . . This balance between the cola can be and is called parallelism'' (Aloysius Fitzgerald, ''Hebrew Poetry,'' NJBC 12:11).

45. For example, the ''Hymn to Christ,'' translated in NTA 2:228–32.

46. For example, the ''Psalms of Thomas,'' translated in NTA 2:498–504.

47. Wellesz, *A History of Byzantine Music and Hymnography*, 149.

48. For example, the Ophite hymn (Origen, *Against Celsus* 6.31; Hippolytus, *Refutation of All Heresies* 5.9.8), the Naassenians' psalm (ibid., 5.10.2), the

Valentinus psalm (ibid., 6.37.6–8), and the hymn of Basileides (Clement of Alexandria, *Stromata* 6.12.81–88).

49. Only a single quotation from this psalter is preserved in the works of Ephraem the Syrian, *Works* 2:483; the historian Sozomen (early fifth century) reports that Harmonius was accomplished in Greek learning, and "was the first to subdue his native language to meters and musical laws" (Sozomen, *Church History* 3.16).

50. I.e., Ignatius, *Letter to Polycarp* (3.2); and fragment 13 from Melito's writings; Kroll, *Christliche Hymnodik*, 19–22.

51. See E. R. Smothers, "Phos Hilaron," *Recherche des science religieuse* 19 (1929) 266–83.

52. Wellesz, *A History of Byzantine Music and Hymnography,* 149.

53. Baumstark enumerates some of these in "Hymns (Greek Christian)," 5–6.

54. Jacques Fontaine, "Les origines de l'hymnodie chrétienne latine," *La Maison-Dieu* 161 (1985) 42.

55. "After water for washing the hands and lamps have been brought in, each is invited to take the floor and sing to God according to his own ability, either drawing upon the scriptures or improvising something of his own" (Tertullian, *Apology* 39).

56. Fontaine, "Les origines de l'hymnodie," 149.

57. The exact role and nature of meter in biblical poetry continues to be a widely debated question; see Aloysius Fitzgerald, "Hebrew Poetry," NJBC 12:16–20.

58. Fontaine, "Les origines de l'hymnodie," 34–35.

59. Clement, *Paidagogos* 3.101.3; for an analysis of the structure of the hymn, see Gerhard May, "Der Christushymnus des Clemens von Alexandrien," in Becker and Kaczynski, *Liturgie und Dichtung,* 1:260–65.

60. Baumstark, "Hymns," 6. Also, see B. Herzhoff, "Zwei gnostische Psalmen: Interpretation und Untersuchung von Hippolytus, Refutatio V.10.2 und VI.37.7," unpublished doctoral dissertation (Bonn, 1973).

61. Wellesz, *A History of Byzantine Music and Hymnography,* 149; this opinion is complemented by that of Bruno Stäblein who believes that Clement was the first Christian to carefully consider the nature of both pagan and Christian music in his time (Bruno Stäblein, "Frühchristliche Musik," *Musik in Geschichte und Gegenwart,* ed. F. Blume (Kassel: Bareureiter-Verlag, 1949–79) 4:1038).

62. Clement of Alexandria, *Hymns,* ed. Alexander Roberts and James Donaldson, trans. W. L. Alexander, Ante-Nicene Fathers 2 (New York: Scribner's Sons, 1926) 296.

63. Kroll, for example, thinks that the hymn had nothing to do with worship (Kroll, *Christliche Hymnodik,* 12), whereas Quasten thinks it perhaps represents "the official prayer of praise of the School of Alexandria" (Johannes Quasten, *Patrology,* 3 vols. [Utrecht and Antwerp: Spectrum, 1950–60] 2:11).

64. It is the metrical construction which, according to Kroll, is the "formal criterion" for defining a hymn in Christian worship (Kroll, *Christliche Hymnodik,* 8).

65. Fontaine, "Les Origines de l'hymnodie," 42; what follows draws upon Fontaine's summary.

66. He continues,

> Why the polemic should have been absent from the writings of early church fathers and so prominent in those of later ones is not easy to explain. . . . Perhaps it was due to cultural factors . . . the attitude of the primitive church might be characterized by simplicity and directness. The later fathers on the other hand, all thoroughly educated in the classical tradition, might be said to have shared the musical puritanism of pagan intellectuals, taking it—for reasons of their own—beyond all precedent. . . . Quasten . . . sees the principal motivation of the patristic polemic as the close association of pagan musical practice with the "pagan cult of idols" (McKinnon, "The Church Fathers and Musical Instruments," 2–3).

67. In central Egypt, about two hundred kilometers south of Cairo, and fifteen kilometers west of the Nile.

68. The fruit of these excavations, led by R. P. Grenfell and A. S. Hunt, have been edited as *The Oxyrhynchus Papyri*, 55 vols. (London: Egypt Exploration Society, 1898–1988).

69. Wellesz's translation reads, "while we hymn Father and Son and Holy spirit let all creation sing amen, amen, amen, Praise, Power . . . to the one Giver of all good things, amen, amen" (Egon Wellesz, "Early Christian Music, Early Medieval Music up to 1300," in *New Oxford History of Music*, vol. 2, ed. Anselm Hughes [London: Oxford University Press, 1955] 4). It is possible that this is not a hymn to the Trinity, but simply a Trinitarian doxology, concluding a hymn that could have had another textual focus.

70. The original publication of the hymn is to be found in *The Oxyrhynchus Papyri* 15 (1922) 21–25. The literature on this musical fragment is vast; for an introduction, see Quasten, *Music and Worship*, 105 n. 59b; a few additional references can be found in Hannick, "Christian Church," NGDMM 4:371.

71. Compare the six transcriptions by various scholars in Stäblein, "Frühchristliche Musik," 4:1053–56.

72. See the useful summary of opinions in Quasten, *Music and Worship*, 105 n. 59b.

73. "The conclusion of this hymn gives no indication of a congregational refrain, and some think that it was meant to be sung by a soloist" (Hannick, "Christian Church," 367); Quasten, on the other hand, thinks this hymn is a witness to the "una voces dicentes" of the early Christian community (Quasten, *Music and Worship*, 70–71).

74. Tertullian, *Concerning Prayer* 27.17.

75. Robert Taft, *The Liturgy of the Hours in East and West* (Collegeville: The Liturgical Press, 1986) 18.

76. For example, the *Odes of Solomon* employ "alleluia" at the close of all but the first two of its forty-two odes; Hippolytus also acknowledges the prac-

tice of reciting "alleluia psalms," to which people respond with "alleluia" (*Apostolic Tradition* 25). Victor Saxer believes that this form was instrumental in the development of responsorial chant in Christian worship; see Victor Saxer, *Vie liturgique et quotidienne à Carthage vers le milieu du IIIe siècle,* Studi di Antichità Cristiana 29 (Vatican: Pontificio di Archeologia Cristiana, 1969) 220.

77. He suggests that the first incontestable evidence is found in the work of Athanasius (d. 373), *Defense of His Flight* 24. Athanasius' language suggests that this responsorial practice is somewhat older, though Caglio would not want to push it much earlier than the end of the third century (E. T. Moneta Caglio, "Lo Jubilus e le origini della salmodia responsoriale," *Jucunda Laudatio* 14-15 [1976-1977] 58-59).

78. Ibid., 5-30.

79. Cattin, *Music of the Middle Ages 1,* 10; also, Helmut Leeb who, reiterating the stance of Jungmann, holds that responsorial psalm-singing was the only form of psalm-singing known to the Church until the middle of the fourth century (Helmut Leeb, *Die Psalmodie bei Ambrosius,* Wiener Beiträge zur Theologie 18 [Vienna: Herder, 1967] 17.

80. Avenary distinguishes seven types of responsorial structures: (1) repetition of every phrase or verse by the choir; (2) intonation by the precentor; (3) a "motto" from the first verse recurring as refrain; (4) "halleluia" as responsorial call; (5) alternate singing of hemistichs; (6) repetition of verses; and (7) additions to the text of psalms (Avenary, "Formal Structure of Psalms and Canticles," 3-6.

81. The term "unison" is used here with some caution, and does not necessarily imply "simultaneous performance of the same pitch, or sometimes at one or more octaves" (*The New Harvard Dictionary of Music,* ed. Don Randel [Cambridge: Belknap Press, 1986] s.v. "unison"), as is usually thought today. "Unison," in the primitive Christian community, could well have been more like heterophony, or "the simultaneous statement . . . of two or more different versions of what is essentially the same melody" (ibid., s.v. "heterophony"). Eliyahu Schleifer, speaking of congregational refrains in synagogues of the talmudic period, provides a useful image in this regard: "the congregation never sings in exact unison, but different members of the congregation sing their own private versions of the melody, which together form a simultaneous rhythmic cloud of variations" (Eliyahu Schleifer, "Jewish Liturgical Music from the Bible to Hasidism," in *Sacred Sound and Social Change: Liturgical Music in Jewish and Christian Experience,* ed. Lawrence Hoffman and Janet Walton, *Two Liturgical Traditions,* vol. 3 [Notre Dame, Ind. and London: University of Notre Dame Press, 1992] 30-31).

82. Tertullian, *Apology* 39.18; further citations can be found in Caglio, "Lo Jubilus," 51 n. 90.

83. For a more thorough discussion of this concept, see Quasten, *Music and Worship,* 66-72.

84. "Therefore it is fitting that you should live in harmony with the will of the bishop, as indeed you do. For your justly famous presbytery, worthy of

God, is attuned to the bishops as the strings to a harp. Therefore, by your concord and harmonious love Jesus Christ is being sung. Now do each of you join in this choir, that being harmoniously in concord you may receive the key of God in unison and sing with one voice through Jesus Christ to the Father" (Ignatius, *Letter to the Ephesians* 4.1-2, trans. Kirsopp Lake, in *Apostolic Fathers*, 2 vols., Loeb Classical Library [Cambridge: Harvard University Press, 1912; rpnt., 1959] 1:177).

85. Clement, *Paidagogos* 2.44, trans. Simon P. Wood in *Christ the Educator*, The Fathers of the Church 23 (New York: Fathers of the Church, Inc., 1954) 132-33.

86. Although "alternating" and "antiphonal" are sometimes considered synonymous, "antiphonal" has many other meanings. See, for example, Bernard Botte, "Antiphona," *Sacris Erudiri* 4 (1952) 239-44.

87. In the "Hymn of Christ" found in the apocryphal *Acts of John*, for example, "amen" is a continuing response; see NTA 2:228-32.

88. Tertullian, *Apology* 39.18.

89. The psalter of Bar-Daisan and his son Harmonius, for example, could have presumed such performance.

90. See the discussion of "Song Forms (Psalms)," above (pp. 78-79).

91. Fontaine suggests that the music for "Phos Hilaron" "must have been melodic and accentual" (Fontaine, "Les origines de l'hymnodie," 41).

92. There is evidence, for example, that the heretical bishop Paul of Samosata (third century) had "choirs" of women singing "hymns" in worship. See the report in Eusebius, *The History of the Church* 7.30.10.

93. James Frederick Mountford and Reginald Winnington Ingram, "Music," *Oxford Classical Dictionary*.

94. Hannick, "Christian Church," NGDMM 4:366.

95. "For temperate harmonies are to be admitted. . . . Chromatic harmonies are, therefore, to be abandoned to immodest revels, and to florid and meretricious music" (Clement, *Paidagogos* 2.4, Ante-Nicene Fathers 2:249). In commenting on this section, Werner goes further and believes one can reconstruct the actual scale used by third-century Christians in Alexandria (Werner, *Sacred Bridge* 1:441-45).

96. McKinnon provides the best compendium of references here in "The Church Fathers and Musical Instruments"; also useful is Robert Skeris, *Chroma Theou: On the Origins and Theological Interpretation of the Musical Imagery Used by the Ecclesiastical Writers of the First Three Centuries, with Special Reference to the Image of Orpheus*, Catholic Church Music Associates, vol. 1 (Altötting, Germany: Alfred Coppenrath, 1976).

97. Harnack, "Christians as a Third Race," *The Mission and Expansion of Christianity*, 266-78.